# All About Katakana

# ALL ABOUT KATAKANA

Anne Matsumoto Stewart

KODANSHA INTERNATIONAL
Tokyo • New York • London

Distributed in the United States by Kodansha America, Inc., 114 Fifth Avenue, New York, N.Y. 10011, and in the United Kingdom and continental Europe by Kodansha Europe by Kodansha Europe Ltd., Gillingham House, 38-44 Gillingham Street, London SW1V 1HU. Published by Kodansha International Ltd., 17-14 Otowa 1-chome, Bunkyo-ku, Tokyo 112, and Kodansha America, Inc.

93 94 95 10 9 8 7 6 5 4 3 2 1

ISBN 4-7700-1696-4

# CONTENTS

# Preface

As useful as it is to casual learners of the Japanese language, and as necessary to serious students, katakana frequently does not receive the close attention that it deserves. The serious student, studying in school where hiragana and kanji maintain pride of place, is often left with a less than perfect introduction to the katakana syllabary. The casual learner (the tourist, business person, etc.), ignorant of katakana's function as a means of transcribing loanwords from English and other languages, remains unaware of its usefulness in acquiring a knowledge of much practical, everyday written Japanese as encountered, for example, in restaurants and hotels. It is for these two divergent types of reader that the present book was written.

One of the primary functions of katakana is for marking native Japanese words for emphasis, much as italics is used in English. Another related function, as mentioned above, is the transcription of loanwords, such as "cake" (*keeki*, ケーキ), "pie" (*pai*, パイ), and "hamburger" (*hanbaagaa*, ハンバーガー). It is such words as this, of which there are a considerable number, that the casual learner will eventually be able to pick up after going through this book. Once the means of transcription has been learned—that is, katakana—the meanings of the words themselves can often (but not always) be deduced by anyone who knows English or whatever other language the word has been borrowed from. Thus the casual learner, with a little effort, will be able to distinguish the names of many "Western food" restaurants and decipher many of the items on the menu, and in general to read and acquire for speaking purposes many words with practical application.

The aim of the present book is thus to teach three things: one, the reading (recognition) of the individual katakana characters; two, the writing of these characters; three, the combination of the characters into actual words. To accomplish the latter end, katakana has been introduced not in the traditional order (which limits the number of words that can be constructed, especially in the primary stage), but in a order that facilitates the building of vocabulary as the student moves from lesson to lesson and adds new characters to his or her repertoire. Exercises are included with each lesson to reinforce and test the reader's mastery of what has been presented to that point.

Following the main text is an appendix of useful vocabulary, categorized for easy reference. Some of these categories concern food, brand names, and barber shops and beauty parlors, areas of particular interest to those making their way through the maze of everyday life in a foreign country. The list of composers, painters, etc., though of less apparent practical use, illustrates the differences between Anglicized and katakana-ized versions of some well-known proper names. The appendix is succeeded by two longish glossaries (katakana-English and English-katakana), which include all the vocabulary items that appear in the book as well as a good deal more. These glossaries will, it is hoped, prove helpful to both casual and serious readers either as practical references or simply as additional vocabulary to be studied at leisure.

Readers who are approaching katakana for the first

time will want to proceed from the Preface to the Introduction for further orientation. More experienced students might decide to go straight to the body of the book without loss, for the basic approach employed there is fairly self-explanatory.

I would like to express my indebtedness to the reference book 「外来語の語源」 吉沢典男 / 石綿敏雄, 角川書店, 1990 (*Gairaigo no Gogen*, by Yoshizawa Norio and Ishiwata Toshio, Kadokawa Shoten), which was of tremendous help in tracking down the origins of many of the loanwords listed in this book. I am also grateful to my editors at Kodansha International, Shigeyoshi Suzuki and Michael Brase, to computer operator Michiko Tsukamoto, and to Jay Thomas, who gave many valuable comments on the first draft. Finally, I wish to extend my sincerest thanks to Mr. Bun K. Aoyama of Tōkai University for his generous help, patience, and constant encouragement during the preparation of this book. His insightful comments have contributed immensely to its final form.

# Introduction

In the historical development of a language, the spoken precedes the written. When a means of recording spoken sounds becomes necessary, it is often borrowed from another language system rather than created from scratch. This is what happened in Japanese. For better or worse, the source of the Japanese writing system is Chinese orthography, with its tens of thousands of ideograms or characters, known as *kanji* in Japanese. Each kanji represents a different word or concept, but does not explicitly show the pronunciation of the word as a sequence of letters as the alphabet does.

Whereas kanji alone are perfectly serviceable in writing Chinese, problems arose when they were adopted by the Japanese, since the two languages are very different. For example, how could the long conjugational endings of Japanese verbs, the individual sounds of which have no meaning of their own, be written in kanji which focus on meaning rather than sound? Although the historical development and reasons are complex and cannot be gone into here, suffice it to say that the Japanese eventually developed two phonetic syllabaries, the curved *hiragana* and angular *katakana*, to overcome the difficulties inherent in using kanji alone. With a few minor exceptions noted later, there is one hiragana and one katakana character for each sound "beat" in Japanese, so that any possible word in the language can be written with either of the syllabaries. There are forty-five katakana characters, as well as several diacritics and a number of combinations.

Kanji, hiragana, and katakana each have different functions. Stated briefly, kanji are used for nouns and the stems of verbs and adjectives, while hiragana are used for conjugational endings and native-Japanese words for which the kanji are obsolete or non-existent. Katakana, the subject of this book, are used in the following cases:

1. For words borrowed from other languages (loanwords), such as *kamera* (camera) and *tenisu* (tennis).
2. For foreign names, such as *Amerika* (America) and *Jonson* (Johnson ).
3. For onomatopoeic and mimetic words, such as *ban* (bang) and *wanwan* (bowwow).
4. For words or phrases, normally written in kanji or hiragana, that are being emphasized; this usage is similar to the use of italics or boldface in English.
5. For the names of plants and animals in academic reports.

In this book we will be concerned with the first two usages, which account for the vast majority of katakana words, but bear in mind that you will probably come across examples of the other usages, which, of course, cannot be "sounded out" as loanwords.

Modern Japanese is thus written in a combination of ideograms (kanji) and phonetic symbols (hiragana and katakana), as the following example shows:

日本製のカメラです。
Nihon-sei no kamera desu. / "It's a Japanese(-made) camera."
[3 kanji, 1 hiragana, 3 katakana, 2 hiragana in that order]

Generally speaking, katakana is gone over rather quickly in most beginning Japanese courses, following a much more thorough study of hiragana. One reason for this is that elementary textbooks are written in hiragana, as are Japanese children's books. Students who have learned Japanese in this manner may realize that their knowledge of katakana is rather shaky and wish to strengthen it, as part of their general study of all forms of written Japanese. This book has been written for such students as this.

Some learners, however, may have no plans at all to master either hiragana or the two thousand or so kanji required for reading a Japanese newspaper. What they want is simply to learn enough Japanese to get along at a very practical, everyday level. Fortunately for this group (especially if they are English speakers), Japanese has many loanwords written in katakana that can be picked up with a minimum of effort. Once this group learns how these loanwords fit into Japanese pronunciation patterns, they will immediately recognize thousands of Japanese words—on the menus of coffee shops, Western-style restaurants, or fast-food chains; at record shops, where music classifications ("jazz" etc.) and non-Japanese artists' names are displayed in katakana; and at countless other places as well.

Anyone with the least familiarity with Japanese will have noticed that loanwords do not usually sound like the source language because of the differences in the pronunciation systems. Moreover, long words and phrases may be truncated, by either deletion (e.g., *suupaa* from "supermarket") or contraction (e.g., *rimokon* from "<u>remote</u> <u>con</u>trol"). Words not ordinarily used together in the original language may be combined in seemingly unusual ways (e.g., *sarariiman*, "salary-man," i.e., male white-collar worker). Such words may not be immediately recognizable. Finally, a loanword may take on a meaning different from that in the original language (e.g., *mama* means "female bar manager" as well as "mom") or may be limited in meaning compared to the range of meanings the word has in the original language (e.g., *sumaato* means "smart" only in the sense of "stylish," not "intelligent").

## Structure of the Book

In this book, katakana characters are not introduced in traditional order (which is shown in Table 1, p. 18). Rather, they are presented in a new order that facilitates the reading and writing of meaningful words from the very first lesson. Lessons 1-4 present the basic katakana one or two at a time, beginning with a demonstration of how to write the characters. With each katakana presented, there is a list of words using that character as well as the characters already presented; the words are transcribed in Roman alphabet, and English glosses are given. Review exercises are provided at the end of each lesson. Lessons 5-8 cover diacritics and other variations and, like the earlier lessons, include word lists and exercises.

Japanese words have been transcribed in the Roman alphabet (*roomaji* ) using a modification of the Hepburn romanization system. Although there are other romanization systems, the Hepburn system was chosen for this book since it is used in most Japanese-English dictionaries. The modification concerns the representation of long vowels: instead of using a macron (e.g., *tōsuto*, "toast"), long vowels are spelled out in full (*toosuto*).

## Using the Book

Although some readers may wish simply to read through the book in order to study katakana for purposes of visual identification, it is recommended that you purchase a square-grid notebook and practice writing each katakana according to the models given. Study (and write, both horizontally and vertically) at least the first three words in the list that accompanies each single or pair of katakana (Lessons 1-4). If possible, study as many of the additional words as possible, to familiarize yourself with words that you will likely encounter in real-life situations. Many of the exercises can also be written down in your notebook. When writing horizontally, write from left to right as you would in English. When writing vertically, start from the upper right corner of the page writing downwards.

When writing katakana (and hiragana and kanji), attention must be paid to the order, direction, and termination of the strokes of a character. In this book, stroke order is indicated by small numbers, and stroke direction by small arrows accompanying the strokes. The importance of stroke order and direction are illustrated by the following pairs of look-alike katakana:

so    n    tsu    shi

There are three ways in which a stroke may be terminated: with a full, firm stop (indicated by an x in the samples), with a tapered stop (indicated by an o in the samples), or with a hook. Hooks appear only in オ, カ, and ホ. Take, for example, the character オ (pronounced *o*):

The first (horizontal) stroke ends in a firm stop, so that it is uniformly thick from beginning to end. The second (vertical) stroke ends in a hook that tapers off to the left and upwards. The third and last stroke begins at the intersection of the first two strokes, proceeds down and to the left and tapers off to a fine point before ending.

Note also that each character is centered in its square and takes up the same amount of space (this is true even when the squares are "imaginary," as when you are writing with ordinary lined and blank paper).

## Pronunciation Tips

Since this book focuses on the Japanese writing system, only the fundamental points of pronunciation are summarized here. The most important thing to remember with respect to learning katakana and loanwords is to ignore the original English pronunciation (or other language) and pronounce the word as the Japanese do. Try to get a native speaker to read the words aloud to you, and avoid relying too much on the romanization, which is intended only as a general guide.

The following are specific points to keep in mind. Small katakana introduced in lessons 7 and 8 (i.e., small ヤユヨァイウエオ) do not take one beat. Only when they are combined with another basic katakana (as in キャキュ ファ, etc.) do they take a full beat. However, ン (n) and small ッ both take a full beat. In this book, a full "beat" corresponds to one katakana letter, except for the small katakana introduced in Lessons 7 and 8:

1. Each "beat" (or more technically, "mora") is represented by a single katakana character (or a regular-sized character followed by certain small ones, as covered in Lessons 7 and 8), and all beats are equal in length and stress, resulting in a level, somewhat staccato rhythm. Loanwords often acquire a larger number of beats than they have in their original language (e.g., "toast," noted above, becomes the four-beat word *to-o-su-to*). Try to give all beats equal length and stress; in particular, avoid squeezing long (double) vowels into a single beat—you could end up with an entirely different word (e.g., *biru* is "building"; *biiru* is "beer").

2. The first letter of a double consonant in the roman-

ized transcription (signified by a small ッ in katakana, introduced in Lesson 5) represents a full beat and must be timed as such. For example, the word *torakku* ("truck" or "track") has four beats, *to-ra-k-ku*. When pronouncing such a word, hold the first consonant of the double consonant for a full beat. To get an idea of what is meant here, note the difference in the duration of the *k* sounds in the word "placard" (where it is spelled with a *c*) and in the phrase "black cat." The pronunciation of the latter resembles the double-k sound in *torakku*.

3. The sound represented by *n* (ン in katakana) before a consonant, an apostrophe and vowel, or the end of a word gets a full beat and is pronounced in four distinct, but related, ways. Pronunciation is as follows: as an "n" before *t*, *d*, and *n*; as "m" before *p*, *b*, and *m*; as "ng" before *k* and *g*; as a nasal sound, as in the French *bon,* at the end of a word or before an apostrophe and vowel.

4. The five vowels of Japanese may be approximated as follows: *a* as in "father," *i* as in "ski," *u* as in "pull," *e* as in "end," and *o* as in "obey." Keep the vowel sounds short.

5. The *r* sound is flapped, much like the sound in the middle of the word "muddy." The sound represented by *f* is actually made with the upper and lower lips slightly puckered (as if blowing out a candle), not with the upper teeth and lower lip as in English.

6. Instead of stressed syllables, as in English, there is high and low pitch in Japanese. This "pitch accent" is symbolized in the romanized transcriptions in this book by the use of boldface type for high-pitched beats and plain type for low-pitched beats. For example, the

Japanese word for "tomato" is transcribed as **to**mato; the first beat, **to**, is pronounced at a slightly higher pitch than *mato*. You will note that in this case (and in many others) the pitch accent falls on a different beat than the stress accent in English. It may help to remember that the first two beats of a word have to be of different pitch, either a high-low or low-high sequence, and that loanwords tend to be pronounced with a high pitch on the third beat from the end of the word (like **to**mato) or on the first beat if there are only two beats.

## The Katakana Tables

The tables in this section summarize all the katakana characters (alone and in combination with one another and with diacritics) that are encountered in written Japanese. You may find it helpful to refer to these tables as you work through the book.

Table 1 indicates the basic katakana syllabary, that is, all the single katakana without diacritics. (These are introduced in Lessons 1-4.) The three katakana in the *w*-row in parentheses (ヰ, ヱ, ヲ) are rarely seen in modern Japanese. ヲ is the direct-object particle *o* and is found only in legal documents (the hiragana を is used for this particle in ordinary writing.) The other two characters are virtually obsolete. The three characters are shown here for completeness and are not covered further in this book.

TABLE 1: Basic Katakana Syllabary

| vowels | | a | i | u | e | o |
|---|---|---|---|---|---|---|
| cons. | 1 | ア a | イ i | ウ u | エ e | オ o |
| k | 2 | カ ka | キ ki | ク ku | ケ ke | コ ko |
| s / sh | 3 | サ sa | シ shi | ス su | セ se | ソ so |
| t/ch/ts | 4 | タ ta | チ chi | ツ tsu | テ te | ト to |
| n | 5 | ナ na | ニ ni | ヌ nu | ネ ne | ノ no |
| h / f | 6 | ハ ha | ヒ hi | フ fu | ヘ he | ホ ho |
| m | 7 | マ ma | ミ mi | ム mu | メ me | モ mo |
| y | 8 | ヤ ya | | ユ yu | | ヨ yo |
| r | 9 | ラ ra | リ ri | ルru | レ re | ロ ro |
| w | 10 | ワ wa | (ヰ) (w)i | | (ヱ) (w)e | (ヲ) (w)o |
| -n | 11 | | | | | ン -n |

Table 2 shows the katakana that take the voicing diacritic ( ゛) and the diacritic that "converts" an *h* sound to a *p* sound (°). (These are introduced in Lesson 6.)

When the voicing diacritic is added to the basic katakana シ and チ (giving ジ and ヂ), the same sound results: *ji*. Likewise, when the voicing diacritic is added to the basic katakana ス and ツ (giving ズ and ヅ), the same sound results: *zu*. Since only one character for each sound is needed in practice, only ジ and ズ are generally used in

18

modern Japanese. ヂ and ヅ are presented in the table for completeness but are not covered further in this book.

TABLE 2: Basic Katakana with Diacritics

|       | a        | i         | u         | e        | o        |
|-------|----------|-----------|-----------|----------|----------|
| **g** | ga<br>ガ | gi<br>ギ  | gu<br>グ  | ge<br>ゲ | go<br>ゴ |
| **z/j** | za<br>ザ | ji<br>ジ | zu<br>ズ | ze<br>ゼ | zo<br>ゾ |
| **d** | da<br>ダ | (ji)<br>(ヂ) | (zu)<br>(ヅ) | de<br>デ | do<br>ド |
| **b** | ba<br>バ | bi<br>ビ | bu<br>ブ | be<br>ベ | bo<br>ボ |
| **p** | pa<br>パ | pi<br>ピ | pu<br>プ | pe<br>ペ | po<br>ポ |

Table 3 shows the katakana that are used in combination with small ヤ *ya*, ユ *yu*, and ヨ *yo* (introduced in Lesson 7). You will notice that, with one exception (デュ *dyu*), all the first katakana are from the *i* column of the basic katakana syllabary. The combination デュ is exceptional because it occurs only in loanwords; it is not really part of the horizontal or vertical series in which it is shown here.

Although these sounds are written with two katakana

characters (one regular-sized and one small), they represent one beat, just like single katakana characters.

TABLE 3: Katakana Used in Combination with Small ャ, ュ, and ョ

|  | **ya** | | | **yu** | | | **yo** | | |
|---|---|---|---|---|---|---|---|---|---|
| **k / g** | kya<br>キャ | gya<br>ギャ | | kyu<br>キュ | gyu<br>ギュ | | kyo<br>キョ | gyo<br>ギョ | |
| **s / j** | sha<br>シャ | ja<br>ジャ | | shu<br>シュ | ju<br>ジュ | | sho<br>ショ | jo<br>ジョ | |
| **ch / d** | cha<br>チャ | | | chu<br>チュ | dyu<br>デュ | | cho<br>チョ | | |
| **n** | nya<br>ニャ | | | nyu<br>ニュ | | | nyo<br>ニョ | | |
| **h / b / p** | hya<br>ヒャ | bya<br>ビャ | pya<br>ピャ | hyu<br>ヒュ | byu<br>ビュ | pyu<br>ピュ | hyo<br>ヒョ | byo<br>ビョ | pyo<br>ピョ |
| **m** | mya<br>ミャ | | | myu<br>ミュ | | | myo<br>ミョ | | |
| **r** | rya<br>リャ | | | ryu<br>リュ | | | ryo<br>リョ | | |

Table 4 summarizes katakana combinations used exclusively for transcribing loanwords. These combinations have been "contrived" by the Japanese in an effort to transcribe foreign words so as to make the pronunciation as close to that of the original language as possible, as opposed to the earlier tendency to reduce pronunciations to the relatively limited syllabary of native Japanese. These combinations (introduced in Lesson 8) employ miniaturized versions of the katakana characters. All the combinations are pronounced as one beat.

TABLE 4: Combinations with the Vowel Katakana

|  | a | i | e | o |
|---|---|---|---|---|
| **w** |  | wi<br>ウィ | we<br>ウェ | wo<br>ウォ |
| **sh / j** |  |  | she je<br>シェ ジェ |  |
| **t(s)/ch/d** | tsa<br>ツァ | ti di<br>ティ ディ | che<br>チェ |  |
| **f** | fa<br>ファ | fi<br>フィ | fe<br>フェ | fo<br>フォ |

Additional combinations continue to make their appearance for the transcription of loanwords and foreign names. While not covered in further detail in this book, the following combinations are listed for reference:

ヴァ *va*, ヴィ *vi*, ヴ *vu*, ヴェ *ve*, ヴォ *vo* are used to transcribe the "v" sound, which does not exist in Japanese (the Japanese pronunciation is a sort of "v" sound made with both lips rather than with the upper teeth and lower lip). In virtually all cases, the katakana of the *b* row (Table 2) are just as acceptable. (For example, "violin" could be rendered as バイオリン *baiorin* or ヴァイオリン *vaiorin*.)

Also make note of the following combinations: クァ *kwa*, グァ *gwa*, クィ *kwi*, クェ *kwe*, クォ *kwo*, トゥ *tu*, and ドゥ *du*.

Table 5 lists several miscellaneous characters that complete the katakana syllabary.

TABLE 5: Other Characters

| ッ (small ツ) | Indicates that the consonant sound of the succeeding character is to be doubled: *kk, ss, tt, hh, gg, zz, jj, dd, bb, pp, tch, ff*. (Lesson 5) |
| --- | --- |
| — (in horizontal writing)<br><br>｜ (in vertical writing) | Indicates a long vowel (p. 26): *aa, ii, uu, ee, oo*. |

The centered dot ( · ) is used to separate elements of a compound word. Note, however, that many times a term that is two words in the source language may be written as one word in Japanese, without a space between the elements.

Part of the fun (and frustration) of katakana is anlayzing a Japanese loanword to try to determine the foreign word from which it was originally derived (which hopefully will aid in understanding the meaning) or trying to synthesize the correct katakana-ization for a foreign proper name which may not yet have an accepted katakana "spelling."

The Japanese language does not contain all the possible sounds found in all foreign languages and therefore there are no equivalent katakana characters for many of the sounds found in foreign words. Often phonetic substitutions or approximations are necessary to represent "unpronounceable" sounds. Although there are no hard and fast rules for substitutions, following are a few of the more common katakana approximations for English sounds not found in Japanese.

• English "l" sound replaced by Japanese "r" sound.
Actually the Japanese "r" sound often more closely resembles an English "l" sound or even an English "d" than an English "r."

    レモン = remon = lemon
    ラリー = rarii = Larry (or rally)

• English "th" sound replaced by Japanese "s" sound.
    スリル = suriru = thrill
    マラソン = marason = marathon

• English "v" sound replaced by Japanese "b" sound.
[Note comments on the katakana character ヴ above.]
    ビデオ = bideo = video
    バレンタイン = barentain = Valentine

• English "er" sound replaced by Japanese long "a" sound.
    ハンバーガー = hanbaagaa = hamburger
    ポスター = posutaa = poster

• English "f" sound is replaced by Japanese "h" sound.
    ホーム = hoomu = (plat)form
    イヤホン = iyahon = earphone

    Please note that the "official/accepted" katakana representation may not always be the best phonetic representation of a word. Accepted "spellings" often have been established through historical precedent and/or based on original language spelling rather than pronunciation.

ホース = hoosu =hose (not ホーズ hoozu)
ニュース = nyuusu = news (not ニューズ nyuuzu)

It is also extremely important to remember that a foreign word, once borrowed, becomes a Japanese word and does not necessarily retain the same meaning(s) or usage of the word in its original language.

For example, two different loanwords can be derived from a single foreign word and have distinct meanings and/or usages attached to each of the new words.

グラス = gurasu = glass (glass cup, used only for whiskey/wine/cocktail glasses)
ガラス = garasu = glass (the material itself, as in a windowpane)

コップ = koppu = cup (drinking glass)
カップ = kappu = cup (coffee/tea cup, trophy cup)

ストライキ = sutoraiki = strike (labor strike)
ストライク = sutoraiku = strike (as in baseball/bowling)

## **Key to Abbreviations and Symbols**

### Origins of Words

| Ch. | = | Chinese | It. | = | Italian |
|---|---|---|---|---|---|
| D. | = | Dutch | Lat. | = | Latin |
| E. | = | English | Port. | = | Portuguese |
| Fr. | = | French | Russ. | = | Russian |
| G. | = | German | Sp. | = | Spanish |

**Note:** English is the language of origin when no specification is made. It is specifically noted only when the Japanese word is derived from an English word or words that differ in meaning or usage from the Japanese word or are a non-idiomatic combination.

### Katakana Writing Samples

o = tapers off
x = firm stop

### Other

An asterisk (✳) indicates a word formed by a deletion or contraction of at least one of the English words or other words listed.

Boldface type indicates high pitch; normal type indicates low pitch (e.g., **to**mato).

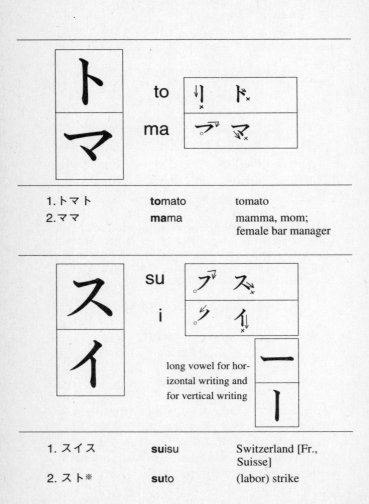

| | to | | |
|---|---|---|---|
| ト | to | | ド |
| マ | ma | ア | マ |

1. トマト **to**mato tomato
2. ママ **ma**ma mamma, mom; female bar manager

| | su | | |
|---|---|---|---|
| ス | su | ア | ス |
| イ | i | ク | イ |

long vowel for horizontal writing and for vertical writing

| ー | | 丨 |

1. スイス **su**isu Switzerland [Fr., Suisse]
2. スト※ **su**to (labor) strike

| | | |
|---|---|---|
| 3. トースト | **too**suto | toast (bread) |
| 4. スー | **su**u | Sue |
| 5. マスト | **ma**suto | mast |
| 6. イースト | **ii**suto | yeast |
| 7. トーマス | **too**masu | Thomas |
| 8. スマート | su**ma**ato | smart (i.e., stylish, slender) |

ku

ri

| | | |
|---|---|---|
| 1. クリスマス | ku**risu**masu | Christmas |
| 2. マイク | **ma**iku | Mike; microphone |
| 3. リスト | **risu**to | list; Liszt |
| 4. リマ | **ri**ma | Lima |
| 5. マーク | **ma**aku | Mark (name); a mark |
| 6. リスク | **ri**suku | risk |
| 7. マスク | **ma**suku | mask (gauze, respirator) |
| 8. クリス | **ku**risu | Chris |

ta

| | | |
|---|---|---|
| 1. タイマー | **ta**imaa | timer |
| 2. トースター | **to**osutaa | toaster |
| 3. スタイリスト | su**tairi**suto | fashion stylist |
| 4. タイ | **ta**i | Thailand |
| 5. タクト※ | **ta**kuto | conductor's baton [G., Taktstock] |
| 6. スター | su**taa** | star (performer) |
| 7. スタート | su**taa**to | start |
| 8. イースター | iisu**taa** | Easter |
| 9. スクーター | su**kuu**taa | scooter |

 n

| | | |
|---|---|---|
| 1. インク | **i**nku | ink |
| 2. スクリーン | su**kurii**n | (movie) screen |
| 3. インスタント | **i**nsu**ta**nto | instant |
| 4. トン | **to**n | ton |
| 5. マトン | **ma**ton | mutton |
| 6. マント | **ma**nto | mantle, cloak, cape [Fr., manteau] |
| 7. タンク | **ta**nku | tank |
| 8. リンク | **ri**nku | rink |
| 9. リンス | **ri**nsu | rinse (for hair) |
| 10. インターン | **i**nta**a**n | intern |
| 11. スタントマン | su**tanto**man | stunt man |

| | | |
|---|---|---|
| ラ | ra |  |

| | | |
|---|---|---|
| 1. ライター | **rai**taa | (cigarette) lighter |
| 2. トラクター | to**raku**taa | tractor |
| 3. ストライク | su**torai**ku | (baseball, bowling) strike (cf. スト, p. 26) |
| 4. リラ | **ri**ra | lira |
| 5. ラリー | **rar**ii | Larry; (car) rally |
| 6. ライト | **rai**to | (stage, car) light(s); lightweight class (boxing) |
| 7. ライス | **rai**su | cooked rice (on a plate, as part of a western-style meal) |
| 8. イラン | i**ra**n | Iran |
| 9. イラク | i**ra**ku | Iraq |
| 10. イクラ | i**ku**ra | salted salmon roe [Russ., ikra] |
| 11. クラス | **kura**su | class |
| 12. クーラー | **kuu**raa | air conditioner, ice chest [E., cooler] |
| 13. トランク | to**ra**nku | (car) trunk |
| 14. イラスト※ | i**ra**suto | illustration |
| 15. スタートライン | su**taatora**in | starting line [E., start line] |

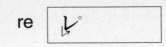

| | | |
|---|---|---|
| 1. レストラン | **re**sutoran | restaurant [Fr.] |
| 2. トイレ※ | **to**ire | toilet, restroom |
| 3. イラストレーター | i**rasutoree**taa | illustrator |
| 4. リレー | ri**ree** | relay (race) |
| 5. レート | **re**eto | rate (of exchange) |
| 6. レース | **re**esu | race; lace |
| 7. レタス | **re**tasu | lettuce |
| 8. タレント | ta**rent**o | TV personality [E., talent] |
| 9. クレーン | ku**re**en | crane (machine) |
| 10. レスラー | **re**suraa | wrestler |
| 11. トレーラー | to**ree**raa | trailer |
| 12. ストレス | su**to**resu | (psychological) stress |
| 13. ストレート | su**toree**to | straight (game score, whiskey) |

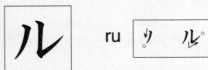 

| | | |
|---|---|---|
| 1. ルール | **ru**uru | rule |
| 2. スタイル | su**tai**ru | (fashion) style; one's figure |
| 3. レンタル | **re**ntaru | rental |

| | | |
|---|---|---|
| 4. レール | **ree**ru | rail |
| 5. スリル | **su**riru | thrill |
| 6. タイル | **ta**iru | tile |
| 7. マイル | **ma**iru | mile |
| 8. マルク | **ma**ruku | mark (Ger. currency; cf. マーク, p. 27) |
| 9. マルクス | **ma**rukusu | Marx |
| 10. リクルート | ri**kuru**uto | recruit |
| 11. トルストイ | to**ru**sutoi | Tolstoy |

---

 fu

---

| | | |
|---|---|---|
| 1. フルート | fu**ruu**to | flute |
| 2. フランス | fu**ransu** | France |
| 3. マフラー | **ma**furaa | muffler; winter scarf |
| 4. タフ | **ta**fu | tough, healthy, sturdy (person) |
| 5. ラフ | **ra**fu | casual attire [E., rough] |
| 6. フリル | **fu**riru | frill |
| 7. リフト | **ri**futo | (ski) lift |
| 8. フライ | **fu**rai | fry |
| | fu**rai** | fly (baseball) |
| 9. フライト | fu**rai**to | (airplane) flight |
| 10. ライフル | **ra**ifuru | rifle |
| 11. インフレ※ | in**fure** | inflation |
| 12. フランクフルト | fu**rankufu**ruto | Frankfurt |

ro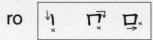

| | | |
|---|---|---|
| 1. ロールスロイス | ro**orusuro**isu | Rolls-Royce |
| 2. クロール | ko**roo**ru | crawl (swimming stroke) |
| 3. フロント | fu**ronto** | front desk (in hotel) |
| 4. ロス※ | **ro**su | Los Angeles; loss; Ross |
| 5. ローラ | **ro**ora | Laura |
| 6. ローマ | **ro**oma | Rome [It., Roma] |
| 7. ローン | **ro**on | loan |
| 8. マロン | ma**ro**n | chestnut [Fr., marron] |
| 9. ロマンス | **ro**mansu | romance |
| 10. ロースト | **ro**osuto | roast |
| 11. ストロー | suto**roo** | straw (for drinking) |
| 12. クローク※ | ku**roo**ku | cloakroom |
| 13. イントロ※ | in**toro** | introduction (musical) |
| 14. ローリー | **ro**orii | Laurie |
| 15. ロータリー | **ro**otarii | rotary |

# Exercise 1

These are the thirteen katakana characters you have learned so far. Can you recognize and read them without looking them up? (Refer to Table 1, p. 18 if necessary.)

|  | vowels | a | i | u | e | o |
|---|---|---|---|---|---|---|
| cons. | 1 |  | イ |  |  |  |
| k | 2 |  |  | ク |  |  |
| s / sh | 3 |  |  | ス |  |  |
| t / ch / ts | 4 | タ |  |  |  | ト |
| n | 5 |  |  |  |  |  |
| h / f | 6 |  |  | フ |  |  |
| m | 7 | マ |  |  |  |  |
| y | 8 |  |  |  |  |  |
| r | 9 | ラ | リ | ル | レ | ロ |
| w | 10 |  |  |  |  |  |
| -n | 11 |  |  |  |  | ン |

## Exercise 2

Write in your notebook the katakana for the following Japanese words. Remember to use the long-vowel mark for double vowels.

1. tomato (tomato)
2. Christmas (kurisumasu)
3. list (risuto)
4. toaster (toosutaa)
5. instant (insutanto)
6. lighter (raitaa)
7. restaurant (resutoran)
8. rental (rentaru)
9. inflation (infure)
10. loan (roon)
11. microphone (maiku)
12. relay race (riree)
13. Frankfurt (furankufuruto)
14. hotel front desk (furonto)
15. rule (ruuru)

## Exercise 3

The following is an ad for a somewhat unusual rental store. Read it and answer the questions below.

| レンタル | |
|---|---|
| 1. スクーター | 6. トースター |
| 2. ロールスロイス | 7. クーラー |
| 3. トラクター | 8. スクリーン |
| 4. トレーラー | 9. マイク |
| 5. クレーン | |

1. What does the store rent? Write the equivalent words in English.
2. You plan to rent a screen, an air conditioner, a microphone, and Rolls Royce. List these items in Japanese in your notebook.

34

mu

| | | |
|---|---|---|
| 1. ムームー | mu**umu**u | muumuu (Hawaiian dress) |
| 2. クリーム | ku**ri**imu | cream |
| 3. トランクルーム | to**rankuru**umu | storage room [E., trunk room] |
| 4. トム | **to**mu | Tom |
| 5. ラム | **ra**mu | rum; lamb (meat) |
| 6. スラム | su**ra**mu | slum |
| 7. ライム | **ra**imu | lime |
| 8. タイム | **ta**imu | time; thyme |
| 9. ムース | **mu**usu | mousse (dessert, hair cream) |
| 10. クレーム | ku**re**emu | complaint (for damages, etc.) [E., claim] |
| 11. フレーム | fu**re**emu | (bowling, eyeglass) frame |
| 12. フルタイム | fu**ruta**imu | full time |

**me**

| | | |
|---|---|---|
| 1. メーター | **mee**taa | meter (gauge) |
| 2. メロン | **me**ron | melon |
| 3. メリークリスマス | **meriikurisu**masu | Merry Christmas |
| 4. メス | **me**su | surgical knife [D., mes] |
| 5. メリー | **me**rii | Mary |
| 6. メイク※ | **me**iku | make-up (cosmetics) |
| 7. メタル | **me**taru | metal |
| 8. メートル | **mee**toru | meter (unit of measure) [Fr., mètre] |
| 9. ラーメン | **ra**amen | ramen (noodles in hot soup) [Ch., lāmiàn] |
| 10. クラスメート | ku**rasumee**to | classmate |
| 11. ルームメート | ruu**mumee**to | roommate |
| 12. トリートメント | to**rii**tomento | treatment (for hair) |

 **ka**

| | | |
|---|---|---|
| 1. カメラ | **ka**mera | camera |
| 2. スカーフ | su**ka**afu | scarf |
| 3. レンタカー | ren**ta**kaa | car rental [E., rent-a-car] |

| | | |
|---|---|---|
| 4. カイロ | **ka**iro | Cairo |
| 5. カフス | **ka**fusu | cuff, cuff link |
| 6. カール | **ka**aru | curl; Carl |
| 7. カラー | **ka**raa | color (TV, photo) |
| 8. カーラー | **ka**araa | curler |
| 9. メーカー | **me**ekaa | manufacturer [E., maker] |
| 10. マイカー | ma**ika**a | privately owned car [E., my car] |
| 11. タンカー | **ta**nkaa | tanker |
| 12. ローカル | **ro**okaru | local |
| 13. カロリー | **ka**rorii | calorie |
| 14. スカート | su**ka**ato | skirt |
| 15. スカンク | su**ka**nku | skunk |
| 16. マスカラ | ma**sukara** | mascara |
| 17. カメラマン | ka**mera**man | cameraman, photographer |
| 18. カレーライス | ka**reera**isu | curry on rice [E., curry rice] |

 a

| | | |
|---|---|---|
| 1. アイスクリーム | **aisukuri**imu | ice cream |
| 2. アメリカ | **amerika** | America |
| 3. アイロン | **airon** | iron (for pressing clothes) |
| 4. メアリー | **me**arii | Mary (also メリー, p. 36) |
| 5. イタリア | i**taria** | Italy |
| 6. アフリカ | a**furika** | Africa |
| 7. アラスカ | a**rasuka** | Alaska |

| | | |
|---|---|---|
| 8. アルカリ | **arukari** | alkali [D.] |
| 9. アクリル | **akuriru** | acrylic |
| 10. アーメン | **aamen** | amen |
| 11. アイライン | **airain** | eyeliner [E., eye line] |
| 12. アラカルト | **arakaruto** | à la carte [Fr.] |
| 13. フレアスカート | **fureasukaato** | flared skirt |

 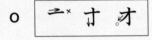

| | | |
|---|---|---|
| 1. オーストラリア | **oosutoraria** | Australia |
| 2. タオル | **taoru** | towel |
| 3. カメレオン | **kamereon** | chameleon |
| 4. ラオス | **raosu** | Laos |
| 5. マカオ | **makao** | Macao |
| 6. カメオ | **kameo** | cameo |
| 7. トリオ | **torio** | trio [It.] |
| 8. オクラ | **okura** | okra |
| 9. オイル | **oiru** | oil |
| 10. オンス | **onsu** | ounce |
| 11. イオン | **ion** | ion |
| 12. ライオン | **raion** | lion |
| 13. オーロラ | **oorora** | aurora (borealis, australis) |
| 14. オカルト | **okaruto** | occult (supernatural) |
| 15. オートレース | **ootoreesu** | auto race |

na

Distinguish from メ (me, p. 36).

| | | |
|---|---|---|
| 1. ナイフ | **na**ifu | knife |
| 2. ナイロン | **na**iron | nylon |
| 3. オーナー | **o**onaa | owner (baseball team, bar, boutique, etc.) |
| 4. マナー | ma**na**a | manners (etiquette) |
| 5. ナイル | **na**iru | Nile |
| 6. マイナス | mai**na**su | minus |
| 7. カナリア | ka**na**ria | canary [Sp., canaria] |
| 8. ナイター | **na**itaa | night game (usually baseball) [E., "nighter"] |
| 9. ランナー | **ra**nnaa | runner |
| 10. トレーナー | to**ree**naa | sweat shirt [E., trainer] |
| 11. ナレーター | na**ree**taa | narrator |
| 12. ナフタリン | na**futarin** | naphthalene, mothball [G., Naphthalin] |
| 13. オールナイト | o**oruna**ito | all-night (usually movies) |
| 14. トーナメント | **to**onamento | tournament |

shi

Align the left ends of all three strokes.

| | | |
|---|---|---|
| 1. シリアル | **shi**riaru | cereal |
| 2. ロシア | ro**shi**a | Russia |
| 3. レシート | re**shi**ito | (cash register) receipt |
| 4. シーン | **shi**in | (movie) scene |
| 5. シール | **shi**iru | sticker [E., seal] |
| 6. シルク | **shi**ruku | silk |
| 7. ナンシー | nan**shi**i | Nancy |
| 8. タクシー | taku**shi**i | taxi |
| 9. シナリオ | shi**nario** | scenario |
| 10. オアシス | oa**shi**su | oasis |
| 11. シアトル | shi**atoru** | Seattle |
| 12. マレーシア | ma**ree**shia | Malaysia |
| 13. アシスタント | a**shi**sutanto | assistant |

 ko

| | | |
|---|---|---|
| 1. コアラ | **ko**ara | koala |
| 2. コカコーラ | **kokako**ora | Coca Cola |
| 3. レインコート | rein**ko**oto | rain coat |
| 4. コーン | **ko**on | corn; (ice cream) cone |
| 5. コレラ | **ko**rera | cholera |
| 6. コルク | **ko**ruku | cork [D., kurk] |

40

| | | |
|---|---|---|
| 7. ココア | **ko**koa | cocoa, hot chocolate |
| 8. スコア | su**ko**a | score |
| 9. コーナー | **ko**onaa | special counter or section (for smoking, specific products, etc.) [E., corner] |
| 10. コーラス | **ko**orasu | chorus |
| 11. コメント | ko**mento** | comment |
| 12. マイコン※ | mai**kon** | microcomputer |
| 13. コースター | **ko**osutaa | coaster (cups) |
| 14. フルコース | furu**ko**osu | full-course (meal) |
| 15. アルコール | a**rukoo**ru | alcohol [D.] |
| 16. アンコール | an**koo**ru | encore |
| 17. フラメンコ | fura**men**ko | flamenco [Sp.] |
| 18. コンクリート | kon**kuri**ito | concrete (cement) |
| 19. コントロール | kon**toroo**ru | control |
| 20. コレクトコール | ko**rekutoko**oru | collect call |
| 21. コーンフレーク | **ko**onfureeku | cornflakes |

サ **sa**

| | | |
|---|---|---|
| 1. サンタクロース | sa**ntakuro**osu | Santa Claus |
| 2. サラリーマン | sa**rari**iman | male white-collar worker [E., salary man] |
| 3. サンフランシスコ | sa**nfuranshi**suko | San Francisco |
| 4. サロン | **sa**ron | salon |
| 5. サイロ | **sa**iro | silo |

| | | |
|---|---|---|
| 6. サイン | **sa**in | signature, auto-graph, signal [E., sign] |
| 7. サイレン | **sa**iren | siren |
| 8. レーサー | **re**esaa | (car) racer |
| 9. サーカス | **sa**akasu | circus |
| 10. サークル | **sa**akuru | circle (i.e., people with a common interest) |
| 11. リサイタル | ri**sa**itaru | recital |
| 12. リサイクル | ri**sa**ikuru | recycle |
| 13. コンサート | **ko**nsaato | concert |
| 14. コンサルタント | ko**nsa**rutanto | consultant |
| 15. サマースクール | sa**maasukuu**ru | summer school |

テ　te

Distinguish from ラ (ra, p. 29).

| | | |
|---|---|---|
| 1. テント | **te**nto | tent |
| 2. アンテナ | an**te**na | antenna |
| 3. ステレオ | su**tereo** | stereo |
| 4. テロ※ | **te**ro | terrorism |
| 5. テーマ | **te**ema | theme [G., Thema] |
| 6. テスト | **te**suto | test |
| 7. テラス | **te**rasu | terrace |
| 8. サテン | **sa**ten | satin [D., satijn] |
| 9. カルテ | **ka**rute | patient's hospital chart [G., Karte] |
| 10. カクテル | **ka**kuteru | cocktail |
| 11. カーテン | **ka**aten | curtain |
| 12. システム | **shi**sutemu | system |

42

| 13. インテリ※ | **interi** | intellectual [Russ., intelligentsija] |
| 14. インテリア※ | **inte**ria | interior decorations |
| 15. コンテスト | **ko**ntesuto | contest |
| 16. ステンレス※ | su**te**nresu | stainless steel |
| 17. コレステロール | ko**resutero**oru | cholesterol |
| 18. ラテンアメリカ | ra**ten'ame**rika | Latin America |

## Exercise 1

The boldface characters are the ten new katakana you have learned in this lesson. Can you read all twenty-three without looking them up? Read across the rows. (Refer to Table 1, p. 18, if necessary.)

| | vowels | a | i | u | e | o |
|---|---|---|---|---|---|---|
| cons. | 1 | ア | イ | | | オ |
| k | 2 | カ | | ク | | コ |
| s / sh | 3 | サ | シ | ス | | |
| t / ch / ts | 4 | タ | | | テ | ト |
| n | 5 | ナ | | | | |
| h / f | 6 | | | フ | | |
| m | 7 | マ | | ム | メ | |
| y | 8 | | | | | |
| r | 9 | ラ | リ | ル | レ | ロ |
| w | 10 | | | | | |
| -n | 11 | | | | | ン |

# Exercise 2

Write in your notebook the katakana for the following words.

1. cameraman (kameraman)
2. car rental (rentakaa)
3. ice cream (aisukuriimu)
4. towel (taoru)
5. knife (naifu)
6. taxi (takushii)
7. antenna (antena)
8. San Francisco (sanfuran-shisuko)
9. concert (konsaato)
10. stereo (suterco)
11. cholesterol (koresuterooru)
12. America (amerika)
13. system (shisutemu)

# Exercise 3

The following chart summarizes what might be found on each floor of a department store:

| | |
|---|---|
| 5F | レストラン、トイレ |
| 4F | ステレオ、トースター、アイロン、カメラ、トイレ |
| 3F | タオル、ナイフ、カーテン、インテリア・コンサルタント |
| 2F | マント、コート、レイン・コート、スカート |
| 1F | スカーフ、マフラー、トイレ |

1 (a) Which floors have a restroom (WC)?
  (b) Where can you find a rain coat?
  (c) Where is the camera department?
  (d) Is there a restaurant? If so, on what floor?
  (e) Which floor has an interior decoration consultant?
2. You plan to buy a towel, curtains, a knife, and a stereo. Write your shopping list in Japanese.

## Exercise 4

Your teacher has collected money for a party this weekend. People with an X before their names have already paid. Who has paid and who hasn't?

| | | |
|---|---|---|
| x ナンシー | x アイリス | マーク |
| スー | ローリー | x サム |
| x ローラ | x リン | カール |
| アリス | テリー | x イアン |
| メアリー | x トム | トーマス |
| アン | クリス | x マイク |
| x ルーシー | x ラリー | アラン |

## Exercise 5

The following bulletin board notice shows Noda-san's business trip schedule and his destinations.

| Noda-san's Schedule | |
|---|---|
| DESTINATION | DATES |
| サンフランシスコ | 4/17 ~ 4/21 |
| シアトル | 4/21 ~ 4/30 |
| フランクフルト | 4/30 ~ 5/8 |
| ローマ | 5/8 ~ 5/13 |
| カイロ | 5/13 ~ 5/17 |
| マカオ | 5/17 ~ 5/22 |

Where is Noda-san on (a) April 18, (b) April 25, (c) May 5, (d) May 10, (e) May 16, (f) May 18?

# LESSON 3

 se

| | | |
|---|---|---|
| 1. セーター | **se**etaa | sweater |
| 2. セーフ | **se**efu | safe (baseball) |
| 3. アクセサリー | **a**kusesarii | (clothing, auto) accessory |
| 4. セール | **se**eru | (bargain) sale |
| 5. セント | **se**nto | cent |
| 6. セスナ | **se**suna | Cessna (plane) |
| 7. セロリ | **se**rori | celery |
| 8. オセロ | **o**sero | Othello |
| 9. センサー | **se**nsaa | sensor |
| 10. セメント | se**mento** | cement |
| 11. アクセル※ | **a**kuseru | accelerator pedal |
| 12. アクセント | **a**kusento | accent |
| 13. コンセント※ | **ko**nsento | wall outlet, wall socket [E., concentric (plug)] |
| 14. ナンセンス | **na**nsensu | nonsense |
| 15. センターライン | se**ntaara**in | center line (road, sports field) |

| | ウ | u |  |

1. ウインク　　　　　**ui**nku　　　　wink
2. カルシウム　　　　ka**rushi**umu　　calcium [D.]
3. アナウンサー　　　a**nau**nsaa　　　announcer
4. ウール　　　　　　**uu**ru　　　　　wool
5. サウナ　　　　　　**sa**una　　　　　sauna
6. ウクレレ　　　　　**ukurere**　　　　ukulele
7. ウイルス　　　　　**ui**rusu　　　　　virus (biological, computer) [G.]
8. レイアウト　　　　rei**au**to　　　　layout
9. アナウンス※　　　a**nau**nsu　　　announcement (over a PA system)
10. カウンター　　　　ka**untaa**　　　(kitchen, sales) counter
11. ウインカー　　　　**ui**nkaa　　　　blinker [E., winker]
12. カウンセラー　　　**ka**unseraa　　counselor
13. タイムアウト　　　tai**mua**uto　　timeout

| | ミ | mi |  |

Distinguish from シ (shi, p. 40). When written quickly, they can look alike.

1. ミルク　　　　　　**mi**ruku　　　milk, coffee cream
2. サラミ　　　　　　sa**rami**　　　salami [It.]
3. セミナー　　　　　se**mi**naa　　seminar
4. ミス※　　　　　　**mi**su　　　　mistake; Miss
5. ミセス　　　　　　**mi**sesu　　　Mrs.
6. ミンク　　　　　　**mi**nku　　　mink

| | | |
|---|---|---|
| 7. ミント | **mi**nto | mint |
| 8. ミシン※ | **mi**shin | sewing machine |
| 9. ミイラ | **mi**ira | mummy [Port., mirra] |
| 10. アルミ※ | ar**umi** | aluminum |
| 11. マスコミ※ | ma**sukomi** | mass media [E., mass communication] |
| 12. マイアミ | mai**ami** | Miami |
| 13. カシミア | ka**shimia** | cashmere |
| 14. スタミナ | su**tamina** | stamina |
| 15. ミサイル | mi**sairu** | missile |
| 16. ミステリー | **mi**suterii | mystery |
| 17. ターミナル | ta**aminaru** | (airport, bus) terminal |
| 18. オートミール | o**otomi**iru | oatmeal |
| 19. ミリメートル | mi**rime**etoru | millimeter [Fr., millimètre] |

 ki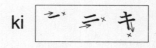

| | | |
|---|---|---|
| 1. キウイ | **ki**ui | kiwi |
| 2. メキシコ | me**kishiko** | Mexico |
| 3. サーロインステーキ | saa**roinsute**eki | sirloin steak |
| 4. キス | **ki**su | kiss |
| 5. スキー | su**kii** | ski(s), skiing |
| 6. キリスト | ki**risuto** | Christ [Port., Christo] |
| 7. テキスト※ | te**kisuto** | textbook |
| 8. テキサス | te**kisasu** | Texas |
| 9. ステーキ | su**te**eki | steak |

49

| | | |
|---|---|---|
| 10. ミキサー | **mi**kisaa | blender; concrete mixer |
| 11. ストライキ | su**tora**iki | (labor) strike (also スト; cf. ストライク, p. 29) |
| 12. ウイスキー | ui**su**kii | whiskey |
| 13. スキーリフト | su**kii**rifuto | ski lift |
| 14. キロ、キロメートル | **ki**ro, ki**rome**etoru | kilometer [Fr., kilomètre] |

 e

| | | |
|---|---|---|
| 1. エスカレーター | e**sukaree**taa | escalator |
| 2. エアコン※ | **eakon** | air conditioner |
| 3. ウエートレス | u**ee**toresu | waitress |
| 4. エラー | e**raa** | (computer, baseball) error |
| 5. エリート | e**ri**ito | elite (person) [Fr., élite] |
| 6. アトリエ | a**torie** | artist's studio [Fr., atelier] |
| 7. エクレア | e**kurea** | éclair [Fr.] |
| 8. エナメル | e**nameru** | enamel |
| 9. エンスト※ | e**nsuto** | stalled engine [E., engine stop] |
| 10. ウエスト | u**esuto** | waist |
| 11. ウエスタン | u**esutan** | western (movie, music) |
| 12. ウエーター | u**ee**taa | waiter |
| 13. エアメール | e**amee**ru | airmail |
| 14. エルサレム | e**rusa**remu | Jerusalem |

| 15. エキストラ | **eki**sutora | extra (in a movie) |
| 16. リクエスト | ri**kue**suto | request (usually songs) |
| 17. イスラエル | i**sura**eru | Israel |

---

 chi

Distinguish from テ (te, p. 42).

---

| 1. チーム | **chi**imu | team |
| 2. コーチ | **ko**ochi | coach |
| 3. ロ－ストチキン | ro**osutochi**kin | roast chicken |
| 4. チリ | **chi**ri | Chile |
| 5. ア－チ | **aa**chi | arch |
| 6. マ－チ | **ma**achi | march |
| 7. ランチ | **ra**nchi | lunch |
| 8. インチ | **i**nchi | inch |
| 9. サ－チライト | sa**achira**ito | searchlight |
| 10. コ－ンスタ－チ | ko**onsuta**achi | cornstarch |
| 11. センチメンタル | sen**chime**ntaru | sentimental |
| 12. センチ、センチメ－トル | **se**nchi, sen**chi-mee**toru | centimeter [Fr., centimétre] |
| 13. スチ－ムアイロン | su**chiimua**iron | steam iron |

---

 ha

---

| 1. ハンサム | **ha**nsamu | handsome man |
| 2. リハ－サル | ri**haa**saru | rehearsal |

51

| | | |
|---|---|---|
| 3. ハンカチ※ | ha**nkachi** | handkerchief |
| 4. ハム | **ha**mu | ham |
| 5. ハート | ha**ato** | hearts (playing cards) |
| 6. ハンマー | **ha**nmaa | hammer |
| 7. ハイカー | **ha**ikaa | hiker |
| 8. ハイフン | **ha**ifun | hyphen |
| 9. ハイテク※ | ha**iteku** | advanced technology [E., high technology] |
| 10. セロハン | se**rohan** | cellophane [Fr.] |
| 11. セクハラ※ | se**kuhara** | sexual harassment |
| 12. ハイライト | ha**irai**to | highlight |
| 13. ウエハース | ue**haasu** | wafer |
| 14. ロースハム※ | roo**suha**mu | roast ham |
| 15. ハーフタイム | ha**afutai**mu | half time |
| 16. インターハイ※ | intaa**hai** | inter high school athletic competition |

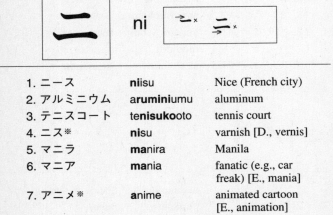

二 　ni

| | | |
|---|---|---|
| 1. ニース | **ni**isu | Nice (French city) |
| 2. アルミニウム | aru**mini**umu | aluminum |
| 3. テニスコート | te**nisukoo**to | tennis court |
| 4. ニス※ | **ni**su | varnish [D., vernis] |
| 5. マニラ | **ma**nira | Manila |
| 6. マニア | **ma**nia | fanatic (e.g., car freak) [E., mania] |
| 7. アニメ※ | **a**nime | animated cartoon [E., animation] |

| | | |
|---|---|---|
| 8. テニス | **te**nisu | tennis |
| 9. ニコチン | ni**kochin** | nicotine [G.] |
| 10. ムニエル | **mu**nieru | buttered fish [Fr., meunière] |
| 11. マカロニ | ma**karoni** | macaroni [It.] |
| 12. ルーマニア | ruu**mania** | Romania |
| 13. スニーカー | su**ni**ikaa | sneaker |
| 14. ミニスカート | mi**nisuka**ato | miniskirt |

---

 **wa**

Distinguish from ク (ku, p. 27).

---

| | | |
|---|---|---|
| 1. ワイン | **wa**in | wine |
| 2. ハワイ | ha**wa**i | Hawaii |
| 3. チームワーク | chii**muwa**aku | teamwork |
| 4. タワー | **ta**waa | tower |
| 5. ワンタン | **wa**n**ta**n | wonton [Ch., wan-tan] |
| 6. ワクチン | **wa**kuchin | vaccine [G., Vakzin] |
| 7. ワイキキ | **wa**i**kiki** | Waikiki |
| 8. アイオワ | ai**owa** | Iowa |
| 9. ワシントン | wa**shi**nton | Washington |
| 10. ワンマンカー | **wa**n**manka**a | bus with driver only, no ticket taker [E., one-man car] |
| 11. カリフラワー | ka**rifura**waa | cauliflower |
| 12. ライフワーク | rai**fuwa**aku | lifework |
| 13. サワークリーム | sa**waakuri**imu | sour cream |

**ホ** ho

| | | | |
|---|---|---|---|
| 1. ホテル | **ho**teru | hotel |
| 2. コンサートホール | kon**saatoho**oru | concert hall |
| 3. ホワイトハウス | ho**waitoha**usu | the White House |
| 4. ホーム※ | **ho**omu | (train) platform; home plate |
| 5. ホース | **ho**osu | (water) hose [D., hoos] |
| 6. ホスト | **ho**suto | host |
| 7. ホイル | **ho**iru | (aluminum) foil |
| 8. ホステス | **ho**sutesu | (bar) hostess |
| 9. ホームラン | ho**omu**ran | home run |
| 10. マイホーム | ma**ihoo**mu | privately owned home [E., my home] |
| 11. マンホール | man**ho**oru | manhole |
| 12. インタホン | **inta**hon | interphone, intercom |
| 13. オクラホマ | o**kura**homa | Oklahoma |
| 14. ホームルーム | ho**omuru**umu | homeroom |
| 15. ホールインワン | ho**oruinwan** | hole in one |

# Exercise 1

The boldface characters are the ten new katakana you have learned in this lesson. Can you read all thirty-three without looking them up? Read across the rows. (Refer to Table 1, p. 18, if necessary.)

| vowels | | a | i | u | e | o | |
|---|---|---|---|---|---|---|---|
| **cons.** | 1 | ア | イ | ウ | エ | オ | |
| **k** | 2 | カ | キ | ク | | コ | |
| **s / sh** | 3 | サ | シ | ス | セ | | |
| **t / ch/ts** | 4 | タ | チ | | テ | ト | |
| **n** | 5 | ナ | ニ | | | | |
| **h / f** | 6 | ハ | | フ | | ホ | |
| **m** | 7 | マ | ミ | ム | メ | | |
| **y** | 8 | | | | | | |
| **r** | 9 | ラ | リ | ル | レ | ロ | |
| **w** | 10 | ワ | | | | | |
| **-n** | 11 | | | | | | ン |

# Exercise 2

Write in your notebook the katakana for the following words.

1. sweater (seetaa)
2. Mexico (mekishiko)
3. the White House (howaitohausu)
4. counselor (kaunseraa)
5. seminar (seminaa)
6. sirloin steak (saaroinsuteeki)
7. escalator (esukareetaa)
8. waiter (ueetaa)
9. steam iron (suchiimuairon)
10. team work (chiimuwaaku)
11. rehearsal (rihaasaru)
12. tennis court (tenisukooto)
13. hotel (hoteru)
14. aluminum (aruminiumu)

# Exercise 3

1. You are at a restaurant with a somewhat unusual selection of dishes. Look at the following menu and translate it into English.

---

### レストラン：クリスタル

アラカルト
1. トースト
2. シリアル
3. オートミール
4. マカロニ
5. ハム
6. カレーライス
7. ラーメン
8. タコス
9. メロン
10. アイスクリーム
11. コーラ
12. ミルク
13. ココア

メインコース
14. サーロインステーキ    15. ローストチキン

アルコール
16. ウイスキー    17. カクテル    18. ワイン
19. ラム

---

2. The following people wish to order the following dishes. Write their orders in Japanese. Okano-san: sirloin steak, slice of melon, whiskey. Yamamoto-san: roast chicken, macaroni, wine. Tanabe-

san: curry on rice, ice cream, cocktail. Maeda-san: oatmeal, toast, ham, cocoa.

# Exercise 4

You see the following sign at a supermarket.

| セール | |
|---|---|
| 1. レタス | 5. トマト |
| 2. セロリ | 6. メロン |
| 3. オクラ | 7. ライム |
| 4. カリフラワー | 8. キウイ |

1. What is on sale today?
2. You need to pick up cauliflower, celery, macaroni, salami, ham, and sour cream (sawaakuriimu). Write your shopping list in Japanese.

# Exercise 5

The following is a list of job openings. Which jobs have already been taken (marked with an X)? Which are still available?

| フルタイム | | | |
|---|---|---|---|
| | 1. ウエーター | X | 6. スタイリスト |
| | 2. ウエートレス | X | 7. イラストレーター |
| X | 3. カメラマン | | 8. カウンセラー |
| | 4. アナウンサー | | 9. アシスタント・コーチ |
| | 5. ナレーター | X | 10. スタントマン |

ne

| | | |
|---|---|---|
| 1. ネクタイ | **ne**kutai | necktie |
| 2. ミネラル | mi**ne**raru | mineral |
| 3. シネマ | shi**ne**ma | cinema [Fr., cinéma] |
| 4. ネル※ | **ne**ru | flannel |
| 5. ネオン | **ne**on | neon |
| 6. アテネ | ate**ne** | Athens |
| 7. ネクター | **ne**kutaa | thick fruit beverage [E., nectar] |
| 8. テネシー | te**ne**shii | Tennessee |
| 9. トンネル | ton**ne**ru | tunnel |
| 10. マネキン | ma**ne**kin | mannequin |
| 11. ハネムーン | ha**ne**muun | honeymoon |
| 12. ラミネート | rami**ne**eto | lamination [E., laminate] |

 so

Distinguish from ン (-n, p. 28), and リ (ri, p. 27).

| | | |
|---|---|---|
| 1. ソフトクリーム※ | so**futokuri**imu | soft ice cream |

| | | |
|---|---|---|
| 2. シーソー | **shi**isoo | seesaw |
| 3. マラソン | ma**rason** | marathon |
| 4. ソロ | **so**ro | solo (music) [It.] |
| 5. ソース | **so**osu | sauce (usually Worcestershire) |
| 6. ソテー | **so**tee | sauté [Fr.] |
| 7. ソニー | **so**nii | Sony |
| 8. ソフト | **so**futo | software; soft |
| 9. ソウル | **so**uru | Seoul, soul music |
| 10. コンソメ | ko**nsome** | consommé [Fr.], clear soup |
| 11. ミネソタ | mi**nesota** | Minnesota |
| 12. クレソン | ku**reson** | watercress [Fr., cresson] |
| 13. ニクソン | **ni**kuson | Nixon |
| 14. ミートソース | mi**itosoo**su | meat sauce (for spaghetti) |

 no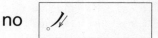

| | | |
|---|---|---|
| 1. ノート※ | **no**oto | notebook |
| 2. ノーコメント | no**okomento** | no comment |
| 3. エコノミークラス | e**konomiiku**rasu | economy class (on planes) |
| 4. ミラノ | **mi**rano | Milano |
| 5. ノルマ | **no**ruma | norm, (assigned) production quota [Russ., norma] |
| 6. イリノイ | iri**noi** | Illinois |
| 7. ホノルル | ho**noru**ru | Honolulu |
| 8. ノーマル | **no**omaru | normal |

9. ノミネート　**no**mi**nee**to　nominate
10. メトロノーム　**me**to**ronoo**mu　metronome [G., Metronom]

---

 mo

---

1. モノレール　**mo**no**ree**ru　monorail
2. エスキモー　e**suki**moo　Eskimo
3. ハーモニカ　ha**amonika**　harmonica
4. メモ　**memo**　memo
5. モカ　**mo**ka　mocha (coffee) [Fr., moka]
6. モナコ　**mo**nako　Monaco
7. サモア　**sa**moa　Samoa
8. レモン　**re**mon　lemon
9. モーター　**mo**otaa　motor
10. モニター　**mo**nitaa　(TV) monitor, consumer tester
11. モスクワ　**mo**sukuwa　Moscow [Russ., Moskva]
12. マンモス　**ma**nmosu　mammoth
13. シナモン　**shi**namon　cinnamon
14. ホルモン　**ho**rumon　hormone [G., Hormon]
15. リモコン※　ri**mokon**　remote control
16. モノクロ※　**mo**no**kuro**　monochrome
17. アンモニア　an**monia**　ammonia
18. モントリオール　**mo**n**torio**oru　Montreal

| | | |  |
|---|---|---|---|

# ケ　ke

| | | | |
|---|---|---|---|
| 1. ケーキ | **ke**eki | cake |
| 2. オーケストラ | o**oke**sutora | orchestra |
| 3. ローラースケート | ro**oraasuke**eto | roller skate(s) |
| 4. ロケ※ | **ro**ke | on location (movie) |
| 5. ケース | **ke**esu | case |
| 6. ケニア | **ke**nia | Kenya |
| 7. ケルン | **ke**run | Cologne (city) [G., Köln] |
| 8. スケール | su**ke**eru | scale (relative size and degree) |
| 9. スケート | su**kee**to | (ice) skating [E., skate] |
| 10. アンケート | an**kee**to | questionnaire [Fr., enquête] |
| 11. ハリケーン | hari**kee**n | hurricane |
| 12. スノーケル | su**no**okeru | snorkel |
| 13. アフターケア | a**futaake**a | aftercare |
| 14. アイススケート | ai**susuke**eto | ice skating [E., ice skate] |

# ツ　tsu

Align the top end of all three srokes.
Distinguish from シ (shi, p. 40).

| | | | |
|---|---|---|---|
| 1. ツナ | **tsu**na | (canned) tuna |
| 2. シーツ | **shi**itsu | (bed) sheet(s) |
| 3. スーツケース | su**utsukee**su | suitcase |

| | | |
|---|---|---|
| 4. ツアー | **tsu**aa | tour |
| 5. スーツ | **suu**tsu | (business) suit |
| 6. ツイン | tsu**i**n | twin (bed) |
| 7. ワルツ | **wa**rutsu | waltz |
| 8. フルーツ | furu**u**tsu | fruit |
| 9. オムレツ | **o**mure**tsu** | omelette [Fr.] |
| 10. オホーツク | oho**o**tsuku | Okhotsk |
| 11. マンツーマン | ma**n**tsuuman | one-to-one [E., man to man] |
| 12. クリスマスツリー | ku**risumasutsuri**i | Christmas tree |

ヒ　hi

| | | |
|---|---|---|
| 1. ヒール | **hi**iru | (shoe) heel |
| 2. ヒーター | **hi**itaa | heater |
| 3. コーヒー | koo**hi**i | coffee [D., koffie] |
| 4. ヒレ | hi**re** | filet [Fr.] |
| 5. ヒント | **hi**nto | hint |
| 6. タヒチ | **ta**hichi | Tahiti |
| 7. ヒステリー | hi**suter**ii | hysteria [G., Hysterie] |
| 8. ローヒール | roo**hi**iru | low-heeled shoes [E., low heel] |
| 9. ハイヒール | ha**ihi**iru | high-heeled shoes [E., high heel] |
| 10. インスタントコーヒー | **insutantoko**ohii | instant coffee |

**ya**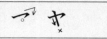

Distinguish from ア (a, p. 37).

| | | |
|---|---|---|
| 1. ヤマハ | ya**maha** | Yamaha |
| 2. イヤホーン | iya**hoo**n | earphone |
| 3. ヒマラヤ | hi**maray**a | Himalaya |
| 4. タイヤ | ta**iya** | tire |
| 5. ハイヤー※ | ha**iyaa** | hired taxi |
| 6. ハレルヤ | ha**reru**ya | hallelujah |
| 7. ロイヤル | **ro**iyaru | royal |
| 8. スノータイヤ | su**noota**iya | snow tire |
| 9. ワイヤレスマイク | wa**iyaresuma**iku | wireless micro-phone |

ユ **yu**

Distinguish from コ (ko, p. 40).

| | | |
|---|---|---|
| 1. ユニホーム | **yu**nihoomu | (sport) uniform |
| 2. ユーモア | **yu**umoa | humor |
| 3. ユネスコ | yu**ne**suko | UNESCO |
| 4. ユタ | **yu**ta | Utah |
| 5. ユニーク | yu**nii**ku | unique [Fr.] |
| 6. ユニセフ | **yu**nisefu | UNICEF |
| 7. ユーターン | yu**uta**an | U-turn |
| 8. ユーモラス | **yu**umorasu | humorous |
| 9. ユーラシア | yu**ura**shia | Eurasia |
| 10. ユースホステル | yu**usuho**suteru | youth hostel |

he

| | | |
|---|---|---|
| 1. ヘアスタイル | **he**a**suta**iru | hairstyle |
| 2. ヘルツ | **he**rutsu | Hertz (cycles per second) [G.] |
| 3. ヘレン ケラー | **he**ren **ke**raa | Helen Keller |
| 4. モヘア | **mo**hea | mohair |
| 5. ヘンリー | **he**nrii | Henry |
| 6. ヘルニア | **he**r**unia** | hernia [Lat.] |
| 7. ヘクタール | **he**k**uta**aru | hectare |
| 8. アフロヘア | **afuro**hea | Afro hairstyle |
| 9. ヘアクリーム | **he**a**kuri**imu | hair cream |
| 10. ヘルスメーター | **he**r**usumee**taa | bathroom scale [E., health meter] |

 yo

| | | |
|---|---|---|
| 1. ヨーヨー | **yo**o**yo**o | yo-yo |
| 2. レーヨン | **re**eyon | rayon [Fr., rayonne] |
| 3. クレヨン | ku**re**yon | crayon [Fr., crayon pastel] |

| ヌ | nu |  |
|---|---|---|

Distinguish from ス (su, p. 26)
and タ (ta, p. 28).

1. カヌー   **ka**nuu   canoe
2. セーヌ   **se**enu   Seine
3. アイヌ   **a**inu   Ainu

# Exercise 1

You have finished all the basic katakana. The boldface characters are the ones learned in this lesson. (Blank spaces inidcate that no katakana exists or the character is obsolete.) Can you read all forty-five without looking them up? Read across the rows. (Refer to Table 1, p. 18, if necessary.)

| cons. \ vowels | | a | i | u | e | o |
|---|---|---|---|---|---|---|
| | 1 | ア | イ | ウ | エ | オ |
| **k** | 2 | カ | キ | ク | ケ | コ |
| **s /sh** | 3 | サ | シ | ス | セ | ソ |
| **t / ch/ts** | 4 | タ | チ | ツ | テ | ト |
| **n** | 5 | ナ | ニ | ヌ | ネ | ノ |
| **h / f** | 6 | ハ | ヒ | フ | ヘ | ホ |
| **m** | 7 | マ | ミ | ム | メ | モ |
| **y** | 8 | ヤ | | ユ | | ヨ |
| **r** | 9 | ラ | リ | ル | レ | ロ |
| **w** | 10 | ワ | | | | ヲ |
| **-n** | 11 | | | | | ン |

# Exercise 2

Write the katakana for the following in your notebook.

1. necktie (nekutai)
2. marathon (marason)
3. no comment (nookomento)
4. remote control (rimokon)
5. monorail (monoreeru)
6. orchestra (ookesutora)
7. questionnaire (ankeeto)
8. cake (keeki)
9. suitcase (suutsukeesu)
10. coffee (koohii)
11. earphone (iyahoon)
12. (sport) uniform (yunihoomu)
13. hairstyle (heasutairu)
14. crayon (kureyon)
15. canoe (kanuu)

# Exercise 3

The following world times are displayed on a series of clocks in a hotel lobby.

| 9 PM | 11 PM | 2 AM | 8 AM | 9 AM | 10 AM | 4 PM |
|---|---|---|---|---|---|---|
| ホノルル | サンフランシスコ | ワシントン | フランクフルト | カイロ | モスクワ | ソウル |
| | シアトル | トロント | ローマ | | | |

1. In which two cities is it 11:00 PM?
2. In which two other cities is it past noon?
3. In which city is it 10:00 AM now?

# Exercise 4

Advertisements for the following companies are shown on the pages listed:

| | |
|---|---|
| ソニー | 49 |
| サンヨー | 52 |
| セイコー | 64 |
| カシオ | 66 |
| ニコン | 73 |
| ヤマハ | 85 |
| トヨタ | 91 |

1. On which page is the Casio ad? The Nikon ad?
2. Which companies are listed on pages 49, 52, and 85?

# LESSON 5

## Double Consonants (Small ッ)

A small ッ is used before a regular-sized katakana character to indicate that the consonant of that character is doubled. The pronunciation of words with small ッ was summarized in the Introduction (pp. 15–16); this character does not have its own pronunciation, but simply takes on the articulation (position in the mouth) of the following consonant sound.

Small ッ is written with the same stroke order as regular-sized ツ (tsu, p. 61). However, in horizontal writing, it is written in the lower half of its real or imaginary square, while in vertical writing it is written in the right half of the square. The samples below illustrate a word with both regular-sized and small ツ.

In this lesson, a longer list of Supplementary Words is provided.

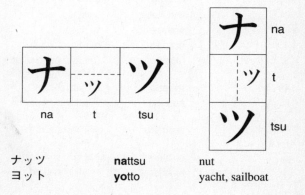

ナッツ      **na**ttsu      nut
ヨット      **yo**tto      yacht, sailboat

| トラック | **tora**kku | truck; track |
| クッキー | **ku**kkii | cookie |
| サッカー | **sa**kkaa | soccer |
| スイッチ | su**i**tchi | (electric) switch |
| ヘルメット | he**rume**tto | helmet |
| リラックス | ri**ra**kkusu | relax |
| ホームシック | ho**omushi**kku | homesickness |
| ネットワーク | ne**ttowa**aku | network |
| コインロッカー | ko**inro**kkaa | coin-operated lock-er [E., coin locker] |

## Supplementary Words

| | | |
|---|---|---|
| 1. マッチ | **ma**tchi | match (for fire) |
| 2. ノック | **no**kku | knock (on a door) |
| 3. コック | **ko**kku | cook, chef [D., kok] |
| 4. ロック | **ro**kku | rock (music); lock |
| 5. ホック | **ho**kku | (garment) hook [D., hoek] |
| 6. ニット | **ni**tto | knitwear [E., knit] |
| 7. ワット | **wa**tto | watt |
| 8. モットー | **mo**ttoo | motto |
| 9. ロッカー | **ro**kkaa | locker |
| 10. ワックス | **wa**kkusu | wax |
| 11. ソックス | **so**kkusu | sock(s) |
| 12. メリット | **me**ritto | merit |
| 13. ラケット | ra**ke**tto | (tennis) racket, (Ping-Pong) paddle |
| 14. ロケット | ro**ke**tto | rocket; locket |
| 15. ステッキ | su**te**kki | (walking) stick, cane |
| 16. ストック | su**to**kku | ski poles [G., Stock] |
| 17. スナック | su**na**kku | bar [E., snack] |
| 18. クラッカー | ku**ra**kkaa | (soda) cracker |

| | | |
|---|---|---|
| 19. ルーレット | **ru**uretto | roulette [Fr.] |
| 20. マスコット | ma**suko**tto | mascot |
| 21. モルモット | mo**rumo**tto | guinea pig [D., marmot] |
| 22. エチケット | **e**chiketto | etiquette |
| 23. クラシック | ku**rashi**kku | classical music [E., classic] |
| 24. カトリック | ka**tori**kku | Catholic [D., Katholick] |
| 25. テクニック | **te**kunikku | technique |
| 26. ハンモック | ha**nmo**kku | hammock |
| 27. マットレス | **ma**ttoresu | mattress |
| 28. ネックレス | **ne**kkuresu | necklace |
| 29. ホッチキス | **ho**tchikisu | stapler [E., Hotchkiss paper-fastner] |
| 30. オートロック※ | **o**otorokku | automatic locking door [E., auto lock] |
| 31. ロマンチック | ro**manchi**kku | romantic |
| 32. ニックネーム | ni**kkune**emu | nickname |
| 33. ノックアウト | no**kkua**uto | knockout |
| 34. ヒッチハイク | hi**tchiha**iku | hitchhike |
| 35. クロワッサン | kuro**wa**ssan | croissant [Fr.] |
| 36. ホットケーキ | **ho**ttokeeki | hotcake, pancake |
| 37. アイスホッケー | ai**suho**kkee | ice hockey |
| 38. クライマックス | ku**raima**kkusu | climax |
| 39. タートルネック | ta**atorune**kku | turtleneck |

# Exercise 1

Write the katakana for the following in your notebook. Write each word both horizontally and vertically. Check the position of small ッ against the samples at the beginning of the lesson.

71

1. yacht (yotto)
2. nut (nattsu)
3. cookie (kukkii)
4. electric switch (suitchi)
5. truck (torakku)

6. relax (rirakkusu)
7. helmet (herumetto)
8. network (nettowaaku)
9. homesick (hoomushikku)
10. wax (wakkusu)

**Note:** Additional exercises that include words with small ッ are found at the end of the next lesson.

# Lesson 6

## Voiced Consonants (ﾞ) and *P* (ﾟ)

The voicing of consonants (e.g., turning an *s* sound to a *z* sound) is accomplished by adding the ﾞ diacritic after a katakana. The katakana of the *h* row of the basic katakana table acquire a *p* sound, which replaces the *h* or *f* sound, when the diacritic ﾟ is added.

## k ➡ g

カ ➡ ガ
ka ➡ ga

| | | |
|---|---|---|
| 1. ガム | **ga**mu | (chewing) gum |
| 2. ネガ※ | **ne**ga | (film) negative |
| 3. ガラス | **ga**rasu | glass (the material) [D., glas] |
| 4. ガソリン | **ga**sorin | gasoline |
| 5. ミシガン | **mi**shigan | Michigan |
| 6. マーガリン | **ma**agarin | margarine |
| 7. フロントガラス | fu**rontoga**rasu | windshield [E., front glass] |

キ ➡ ギ
ki ➡ gi

| | | |
|---|---|---|
| 1. ギター | **gi**taa | guitar |
| 2. ギフト | **gi**futo | gift |
| 3. イギリス | i**giri**su | United Kingdom [Port., Inglez] |

| 4. アレルギー | **are**rugii | allergy [G., Allergie] |
| 5. エネルギー | **ene**rugii | energy [G., Energie] |

## ク → グ
## ku → gu

| 1. グラス | **gu**rasu | liquor (beer, whiskey, wine) glass (cf., ガラス above) |
| 2. グルメ | **gu**rume | gourmet [Fr.] |
| 3. カタログ | ka**tarogu** | catalog |
| 4. スモッグ | su**mo**ggu | smog |
| 5. ヨーグルト | yoo**gu**ruto | yogurt |
| 6. イヤリング | **i**yaringu | earring |
| 7. グロテスク | **gu**ro**te**suku | grotesque [Fr.] |

## ケ → ゲ
## ke → ge

| 1. ゲーム | **ge**emu | game (other than sports) |
| 2. ゲリラ | **ge**rira | guerrilla [Sp.] |
| 3. ゲスト | **ge**suto | guest |
| 4. ゲート | **ge**eto | (airport, horse race starting) gate |
| 5. ゲーテ | **ge**ete | Goethe |
| 6. レントゲン | ren**to**gen | X-ray [G., Röntgen] |
| 7. ゲームセンター | **ge**e**muse**ntaa | video arcade [E., game center] |

## コ → ゴ
## ko → go

| 1. ゴム | **go**mu | rubber [D., gom] |
| 2. ゴルフ | **go**rufu | golf |

| | | |
|---|---|---|
| 3. ゴリラ | **go**rira | gorilla |
| 4. タンゴ | **ta**ngo | tango |
| 5. シカゴ | shi**ka**go | Chicago |
| 6. オルゴール | **o**rugooru | music box [D., orgel] |
| 7. エゴイスト | e**goi**suto | egoist, egotist |

# s / sh ➡ z / j

## サ ➡ ザ
## sa ➡ za

| | | |
|---|---|---|
| 1. レーザー | **ree**zaa | laser |
| 2. ターザン | **ta**azan | tarzan |
| 3. クレンザー | ku**ren**zaa | cleanser |
| 4. クルーザー | ku**ruu**zaa | (cabin) cruiser |
| 5. オンザロック | **onza**rokku | on the rocks |
| 6. シンセサイザー | shi**nsesa**izaa | synthesizer |
| 7. インフルエンザ | **infurue**nza | influenza |

## シ ➡ ジ
## shi ➡ ji

| | | |
|---|---|---|
| 1. レジ※ | **re**ji | cash register |
| 2. ラジオ | **ra**jio | radio |
| 3. アジア | **a**jia | Asia |
| 4. イメージ | **imee**ji | image |
| 5. オレンジ | **ore**nji | orange (color, fruit) |
| 6. ジグザグ | **ji**guzagu | zigzag |
| 7. メッセージ | **messee**ji | message |

## ス ➡ ズ
## su ➡ zu

| | | |
|---|---|---|
| 1. チーズ | **chi**izu | cheese |
| 2. サイズ | **sa**izu | size |
| 3. レンズ | **re**nzu | lens |

| | | | |
|---|---|---|---|
| 4. ジーンズ | **ji**inzu | jeans | |
| 5. マヨネーズ | ma**yone**ezu | mayonnaise [Fr.] | |
| 6. フリーサイズ | fur**iisa**izu | one size fits all [E., free size] | |
| 7. コンタクトレンズ | ko**ntakutore**nzu | contact lens | |

セ ➡ ゼ
se ➡ ze

---

| | | |
|---|---|---|
| 1. ゼロ | **ze**ro | zero [Fr., zéro] |
| 2. ゼリー | **ze**rii | gelatin dessert [E., jelly] |
| 3. ゼラチン | **zerachin** | gelatin (substance) |
| 4. ゼッケン | **ze**kken | athlete's shirt number [G., Zeichen] |
| 5. ノイローゼ | no**iro**oze | neurosis, nervous breakdown [G., Neurose] |
| 6. アルゼンチン | aru**ze**nchin | Argentina |
| 7. ロサンゼルス | ro**sanze**rusu | Los Angeles |

ソ ➡ ゾ
so ➡ zo

---

| | | |
|---|---|---|
| 1. ゾーン | **zo**on | zone |
| 2. リゾート | ri**zo**oto | resort |
| 3. アマゾン | a**mazon** | Amazon |
| 4. アリゾナ | ar**izona** | Arizona |

# t ➡ d

タ ➡ ダ
ta ➡ da

---

| | | |
|---|---|---|
| 1. ダム | **da**mu | dam |
| 2. ダイヤ※ | **da**iya | diamond; train or plane timetable [E., diagram] |

| 3. ユダヤ | **yu**daya | Judea, Jewish [Lat., Judaea] |
| 4. サラダ | **sa**rada | salad |
| 5. オランダ | or**anda** | Holland [Port., Olanda] |
| 6. カレンダー | kar**en**daa | calendar |
| 7. キーホルダー | kii**ho**rudaa | key chain [E., key holder] |

テ ➡ デ
te ➡ de

| 1. デモ※ | **de**mo | demonstration (protest) |
| 2. データ | **dee**ta | data |
| 3. デート | **dee**to | date (boy-girl) |
| 4. デザート | de**zaa**to | dessert |
| 5. デジタル | **de**jitaru | digital |
| 6. ゲレンデ | ge**rende** | ski slope [G., Gelände] |
| 7. デザイナー | de**za**inaa | designer |

ト ➡ ド
to ➡ do

| 1. ドル | **do**ru | dollar [D.] |
| 2. ドイツ | **do**itsu | Germany [D., Duits] |
| 3. ガード | **ga**ado | guard; railroad trestle [E., girder (bridge)] |
| 4. ドーナツ | **do**onatsu | doughnut |
| 5. アイドル | **ai**doru | popular teenage singer [E., idol] |
| 6. アイルランド | ai**ruran**do | Ireland |
| 7. インドネシア | in**done**shia | Indonesia |

# h / f ➡ b

ハ ➡ バ
ha ➡ ba

| | | | |
|---|---|---|---|
| 1. | バス | **ba**su | bus; bath; bass (vocal part) |
| 2. | バター | **ba**taa | butter |
| 3. | バイキング | **ba**ikingu | buffet [E., Viking] |
| 4. | オートバイ※、バイク | ooto**ba**i, **ba**iku | motorcycle [E., auto bicycle] |
| 5. | バーコード | **ba**akoodo | bar code |
| 6. | アルバイト、バイト※ | aru**ba**ito, **ba**ito | side job [G., Arbeit] |
| 7. | ハンバーガー | han**ba**agaa | hamburger |

ヒ ➡ ビ
hi ➡ bi

| | | | |
|---|---|---|---|
| 1. | ビザ | **bi**za | visa |
| 2. | ビル※ | **bi**ru | concrete building; Bill |
| 3. | ビール | **bi**iru | beer [D., bier] |
| 4. | ビデオ | **bi**deo | video |
| 5. | テレビ※ | te**re**bi | television |
| 6. | リハビリ※ | ri**habi**ri | rehabilitation |
| 7. | ビニールハウス | **bi**niiruhausu | plastic greenhouse [E., vinyl house] |

フ ➡ ブ
fu ➡ bu

| | | | |
|---|---|---|---|
| 1. | ブーケ | **bu**uke | bouquet [Fr.] |
| 2. | ブーム | **bu**umu | boom, fad |
| 3. | テーブル | tee**bu**ru | table (furniture) |
| 4. | ブラジル | **bu**rajiru | Brazil |
| 5. | オーブン | oo**bu**n | oven |
| 6. | ブローカー | **bu**rookaa | broker |

|   |   |   |
|---|---|---|
| 7. サイドブレーキ | sai**dobure**eki | hand/parking brake [E., side brake] |

へ → ベ
he → be

|   |   |   |
|---|---|---|
| 1. ベル | **be**ru | bell |
| 2. ベルギー | **be**rugii | Belgium |
| 3. ベトナム | **betonamu** | Vietnam |
| 4. ベビーカー | **bebii**kaa | stroller [E., baby car] |
| 5. ベッドタウン | be**ddotau**n | bedroom community, suburbs [E., bed town] |
| 6. シートベルト | shii**tobe**ruto | seat belt |
| 7. エレベーター | e**rebe**etaa | elevator |

ホ → ボ
ho → bo

|   |   |   |
|---|---|---|
| 1. ボタン | **bo**tan | button [Port., botão] |
| 2. リボン | ri**bo**n | ribbon |
| 3. ズボン | zu**bo**n | trousers, pants [Fr., jupon] |
| 4. ボーナス | **bo**onasu | bonus |
| 5. ロボット | ro**bo**tto | robot |
| 6. サボテン | sa**bo**ten | cactus [Sp., sapoten] |
| 7. バレーボール | ba**reebo**oru | volleyball |

# h / f → p

ハ → パ
ha → pa

|   |   |   |
|---|---|---|
| 1. パン | **pa**n | bread [Port., pão] |
| 2. パーマ※ | **pa**ama | permanent wave, perm |

| | | |
|---|---|---|
| 3. スーパー※ | **su**upaa | supermarket; movie subtitle [E., superimpose] |
| 4. デパート※ | de**paa**to | department store |
| 5. パーセント | paa**se**nto | percent |
| 6. フライパン※ | fu**raipan** | frying pan |
| 7. パート、パートタイム | **paa**to, paa**tota**imu | part-time |

## ヒ → ピ
### hi → pi

| | | |
|---|---|---|
| 1. ピアノ | pi**ano** | piano |
| 2. コピー | **ko**pii | copy (usually photocopy) |
| 3. ピーマン | **pi**iman | green pepper [Fr., piment] |
| 4. スピーチ | su**pi**ichi | speech |
| 5. アスピリン | a**supirin** | aspirin |
| 6. ピーナッツ | **pi**inattsu | peanut |
| 7. オリンピック | o**rinpi**kku | the Olympics |

## フ → プ
### fu → pu

| | | |
|---|---|---|
| 1. プロ※ | **pu**ro | professional; (movie) production |
| 2. プール | **pu**uru | (swimming) pool |
| 3. ギプス | **gi**pusu | plaster cast [D., gips] |
| 4. グループ | gu**ruu**pu | group |
| 5. ワープロ※ | waa**puro** | word processor |
| 6. プレゼント | pu**re**zento | present (gift) |
| 7. プログラム | pu**rogu**ramu | program |

## ヘ → ペ
### he → pe

| | | |
|---|---|---|
| 1. ペア | **pe**a | pair (two people) |

| 2. ペット | **pe**tto | pet (animal) |
| 3. オペラ | **o**pera | opera [It.] |
| 4. ペンキ | **pe**n**ki** | house paint [D., pek] |
| 5. スペイン | su**pe**in | Spain |
| 6. ボールペン※ | bo**orupen** | ballpoint pen |
| 7. トイレットペーパー | to**irettope**e**paa** | toilet paper |

ホ ➡ ポ
ho ➡ po

---

| 1. ポスト | **po**suto | post (position); mail box (on street corner) |
| 2. スポーツ | su**po**otsu | sport |
| 3. パスポート | pa**supo**oto | passport |
| 4. プロポーズ | pu**ropo**ozu | marriage proposal [E., propose] |
| 5. ポータブル | **po**otaburu | portable |
| 6. シンポジウム | shin**poji**umu | symposium |
| 7. ポケットベル、 | po**ketto**be**ru**, | pager, beeper |
| ポケベル※ | po**kebe**ru | [E., pocket bell] |

# Exercise 1

The following buttons are found on a beverage vending machine.

| ソーダ | アイスコーヒー | ホットコーヒー |
|---|---|---|
| 1. コカコーラ | 6. ブラック | 10. ブラック |
| 2. ペプシ | 7. クリーム | 11. クリーム |
| 3. セブンアップ | 8. シロップ | 12. 砂糖 (satoo=sugar) |
| 4. グレープ | 9. シロップ＋ | 13. 砂糖＋クリーム |
| 5. オレンジ | クリーム | |

Which button would you press to get the following drinks?

Hot coffee with cream
Iced coffee, black
Iced coffee with syrup
Seven-Up
Grape soda

## Exercise 2

You and your friends are planning to participate in some Sports Day events. Look at the list below and sign up for your friends. Write both the person's name and the sport he or she wishes to play.

| バレーボール | アイスホッケー |
|---|---|
| バスケットボール | ゴルフ |
| サッカー | ボウリング |
| ラグビー | ピンポン |

1. Bill (biru) wants to play basketball.
2. Robert (robaato) wants to play rugby.
3. Douglas (dagurasu) wants to play golf.
4. Peter (piitaa) wants to play ice hockey.
5. Paul (pooru) wants to play soccer.
6. Diane (daian) wants to play volleyball.
7. Susan (suuzan) wants to play ping-pong.
8. Elizabeth (erizabesu) wants to bowl (bowling).

# LESSON 7

## Combinations with Small *Ya*, *Yu*, and *Yo* (ヤ, ユ, ヨ)

Small *ya* ヤ, *yu* ユ, and *yo* ヨ may be added to katakana of the *i* column (i.e., キ, シ, チ, etc.; see Table 1, p. 18). The result, pronounced as a single beat, is spoken as a combination of the consonant of the *i*-column katakana and *ya*, *yu*, or *yo*. For example, キ *ki* + ヤ(small) *ya* = キャ *kya*. In some cases, the combination is such that the pronunciation is more clearly indicated in romanization with an *h* or no additional letter, rather than a *y*:

シ shi + ヤ／ユ／ヨ = シャ sha ／ シュ shu ／ ショ sho
ジ ji + ヤ／ユ／ヨ = ジャ ja ／ ジュ ju ／ ジョ jo
チ chi + ヤ／ユ／ヨ = チャ cha ／ チュ chu ／ チョ cho

A combination not involving a katakana character of the *i* column is デュ *dyu*.

As with small ッ, small ヤ, ユ, and ヨ are written in the lower half of their real or imaginary square in horizontal writing, and in the right half of the square in vertical writing. A writing sample is included at the beginning of each of the word lists below.

### Words with ヤ

In practice, few if any loanwords happen to include the beats ニャ *nya*, ヒャ *hya*, ビャ *bya*, ピャ *pya*, ミャ *mya*, or リャ *rya*, so none are shown below.

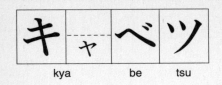

kya be tsu

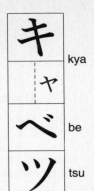

kya
be
tsu

キャベツ      **kya**betsu     cabbage

### キャ kya

| | | |
|---|---|---|
| キャンプ | **kya**npu | camp |
| キャンセル | **kya**nseru | cancel, cancellation |

### ギャ gya

| | | |
|---|---|---|
| ギャラリー | **gya**rarii | (art) gallery, spectators (at a sporting event) |
| ギャンブル | **gya**nburu | gamble, gambling |

### シャ sha

| | | |
|---|---|---|
| ワイシャツ※ | wai**sha**tsu | dress shirt [E., white shirt] |
| イニシャル | ini**sha**ru | (one's) initials |

### ジャ ja

| | | |
|---|---|---|
| ジャム | **ja**mu | (fruit) jam |
| マネージャー | ma**nee**jaa | (store) manager |

| ケチャップ | ke**cha**ppu | ketchup |
| チャンピオン | **cha**npion | champion |

## Words with ユ

All possible combinations of *i*-column katakana and ユ appear in loanwords, as does the combination デュ *dyu*.

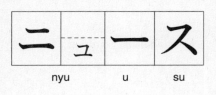

nyu　　　u　　　su

ニュース　　　**nyu**usu　　　news

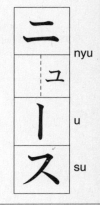

nyu

u

su

### キュ kyu

| バーベキュー | ba**abe**kyuu | barbecue |
| マニキュア | ma**nikyua** | nail polish [E., manicure] |

### ギュ gyu

| レギュラー | **re**gyuraa | regular (member) |

### シュ shu

| ラッシュアワー | ra**sshua**waa | rush hour |
| キャッシュカード | kya**sshuka**ado | cash card |

## ジュ ju

| ジュース | **ju**usu | juice |
| スケジュール | su**ke**juuru | schedule |

## チュ chu

| シチュー | shi**chu**u | stew |
| アマチュア | a**machu**a | amateur |

## デュ dyu

| デュエット | **dyu**etto | duet |
| プロデューサー | pu**rodyu**usaa | producer |

## ニュ nyu

| メニュー | **me**nyuu | menu |
| マニュアル | ma**nyuaru** | manual (handbook) |

## ヒュ hyu

| ヒューズ | **hyu**uzu | fuse |

## ビュ byu

| インタビュー | **i**ntabyuu | interview |
| デビュー | **de**byuu | debut [Fr., début] |

## ピュ pyu

| ポピュラー | **po**pyuraa | popular (music) |
| コンピュータ(ー) | kon**pyu**uta(a) | computer |

## ミュ myu

| ミュージカル | **myu**ujikaru | musical (play) |

| ボリューム | **boryuumu** | volume (sound, amount) |
| リューマチ | **ryuumachi** | rheumatism [D., Rheumatisch] |

## Words with ョ

In practice, few if any loanwords happen to include the beats キョ *kyo*, ギョ *gyo*, ニョ *nyo*, ヒョ *hyo*, ビョ *byo*, ピョ *pyo*, ミョ *myo*, or リョ *ryo*, so none are shown below.

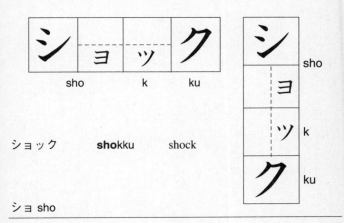

ショック　　　　**sho**kku　　　shock

ショ sho

| クッション | **ku**sshon | cushion |
| ローション | **ro**oshon | lotion |
| マンション | **ma**nshon | condominium [E., mansion] |
| ショールーム | sho**oru**umu | showroom |
| コミュニケーション | ko**myunikee**shon | communication |

## ジョ jo

| ジョージ | **jo**oji | George |
| ジョッキ | **jo**kki | beer mug [E., jug] |
| ジョギング | jo**gingu** | jogging |

## チョ cho

| チョーク | **cho**oku | chalk |
| チョコレート | cho**koree**to | chocolate |

## Exercise 1

The following is a menu from an ice cream shop. Read it and write the orders in your notebook, following the example. Try ordering chocolate ice cream, double/cup; raspberry sherbet, single/cone; rainbow sherbet, single/cup; rocky road ice cream, double/cone.

メニュー

| アイスクリーム | シャーベット | コーン | |
|---|---|---|---|
| バニラ | オレンジ | シングル | ¥220 |
| ストロベリー | ラズベリー | ダブル | ¥350 |
| チョコレート | レモン | | |
| ラムレーズン | ライム | カップ | |
| モカチップ | パイナップル | シングル | ¥200 |
| マカデミアナッツ | メロン | ダブル | ¥330 |
| ロッキーロード | レインボー | | |

オーダー

Vanilla ice cream,
single / cone      バニラアイスクリーム　シングル／コーン

## Exercise 2

The following chart at a record shop shows the aisle location for various types of music.

| レコード、カセット・テープ、ビデオ・テープ | | |
|---|---|---|
| クラシック | 1 | ショパン、ベートーベン、バッハ |
| オペラ／バレエ | 2 | チャイコフスキー、ワーグナー、シューベルト |
| ジャズ | 3 | デューク・エリングトン |
| ロック | 4 | ビートルズ、エルビス・プレスリー、マイケル・ジャクソン |
| ポピュラー | 5 | フランク・シナトラ、レイ・チャールズ |
| ミュージカル | 6 | キャッツ |

1. What category of music is found in each aisle?
2. You want to find records, tapes, or CDs for Wagner, Frank Sinatra, Bach, Duke Ellington, Tchaikovsky, Chopin, Michael Jackson, Cats, and Schubert. To which aisle should you go to?

baha

| Name | Aisle | Type |
|---|---|---|
| Wagner | ワーグナー 2 | オペラ／バレエ (opera/ballet) |

# Exercise 3

You plan to order a pizza for your party.
1. Tell people what toppings are available, based on the following menu.
2. The majority want pepperoni, black olive, mushroom, onion, and double cheese. Write down the order in katakana. Everyone definitely is against ordering anchovy. Write that down also in katakana.

---

### トッピング・メニュー

ベーコン、ペパロニ、ソーセージ、サラミ、ハム、ツ
ナ、アンチョビ、ブラックオリーブ、マッシュルーム、
オニオン、ピーマン、コーン、ダブルチーズ

---

# LESSON 8 ⸺

## Combinations with Small Vowel Katakana

Written small, the five vowels (ア, イ, ウ, エ, オ) are used
after other katakana to transcribe sound combinations that do
not exist in native Japanese (i.e., that cannot be transcribed
with the single or double katakana introduced so far). Each
such combination takes a full beat. As with small ャ, ュ, and
ョ, these vowels are written in the lower half of the real or
imaginary square in horizontal writing, and in the right half
in vertical writing. A sample is included at the beginning of
the word list for each of the small vowel katakana. (In practice, few words with small ゥ exist, so none are included in
the lists below.)

**Words with ア**  ⸺

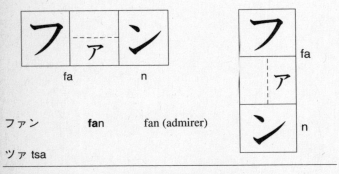

| ファン | **fa**n | fan (admirer) |
|---|---|---|

ツァ tsa

モーツァルト     **mo**otsaruto     Mozart

| ファイト | **fa**ito | fighting spirit, fervor [E., fight] |
| ファイル | **fa**iru | file (papers) |
| ソファー | **so**faa | sofa |
| ファ(ッ)クス | **fa**k(k)usu | fax |
| ファッション | **fa**sshon | fashion |
| アルファベット | aru**fabe**tto | alphabet |

## Words with イ

di　　　su　　　ko

ディスコ　　**di**suko　　disco

| ウィーン | **wi**in | Vienna [G., Wien] |
| ゴールデンウィーク | gooruden**wi**iku | Golden Week holidays (Apr. 29–May 5) |

| パーティー | **pa**atii | party |
| アイスティー | ai**su**tii | iced tea |
| ティーシャツ | ti**ishatsu** | T-shirt |

| ボランティア | **bora**ntia | volunteer |
| コミュニティー | **komyu**nitii | community |
| マーケティング | **maa**ketingu | marketing |

## ディ di

| キャディー | **kya**dii | (golf) caddie |
| オーディオ | **oo**dio | audio |
| メロディー | **mero**dii | melody |
| コメディアン | **kome**dian | comedian |
| ボディービル※ | **bodiibi**ru | body-building |
| レーザーディスク | **reezaadi**suku | laser disc |
| ディズニーランド | **dizuniira**ndo | Disneyland |

## フィ fi

| フィルム | **firu**mu | film (roll) |
| フィナーレ | **fina**are | finale (stage show) [It.] |
| フィアンセ | **fia**nse | fiancé , fiancée [Fr.] |
| フィリピン | **firi**pin | the Philippines |
| トロフィー | **toro**fii | trophy |
| サーフィング | **saa**fingu | surfing |

## Words with エ

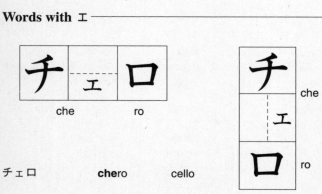

| チェロ | **che**ro | cello |

94

## ウェ we

| | | |
|---|---|---|
| ノルウェー | **no**ruwee | Norway |
| ロープウェー | ro**opuwee** | suspended cable car [E., rope way] |
| スキーウェア | su**kiiwe**a | skiwear |
| ウェディングドレス | we**dingudo**resu | wedding dress |

## シェ she

| | | |
|---|---|---|
| シェリー | **she**rii | sherry |
| シェークスピア | she**ekusu**pia | Shakespeare |

## ジェ je

| | | |
|---|---|---|
| プロジェクト | pu**ro**jekuto | a project |
| ジェットコースター | je**ttoko**osutaa | roller coaster [E., jet coaster] |

## チェ che

| | | |
|---|---|---|
| チェス | **che**su | chess |
| チェーン | **che**en | chain |
| チェックアウト | che**kkua**uto | checkout |
| ボディーチェック | bo**diiche**kku | body search / frisk [E., body check] |

## フェ fe

| | | |
|---|---|---|
| フェリー | **fe**rii | ferry |
| カフェイン | ka**fe**in | caffeine [G., Kaffein] |
| フェミニスト | fe**mini**suto | gallant man; feminist |
| アイスクリームパフェ | a**isukuriimupa**fe | ice cream parfait |

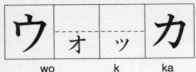

| ウォッカ | **wo**kka | vodka [R.] |

### ウォ wo

| ウォークマン | **wo**okuman | Walkman |
| ミネラルウォーター | mineraru**wo**otaa | mineral water |
| ストップウォッチ | sutoppu**wo**tchi | stopwatch |

### フォ fo

| フォーク | **fo**oku | fork; folk music |
| リフォーム | ri**fo**omu | major alterations to clothing or a home [E., reform] |
| シンフォニー | shin**fo**nii | symphony |
| インフォーマル | in**fo**omaru | informal |
| カリフォルニア | kari**fo**runia | California |
| フォークソング | **fo**oku**so**ngu | folk song |
| インフォメーション | in**fo**meeshon | information (desk) |

## Exercise 1

Look at the following timetable and see what's on TV tonight.

| プログラム | | |
|---|---|---|
| チャンネル | | |
| 2 | 5 | 9 |
| 6:00 ローカル ニュース | ワールド ニュース | ミスユニバース コンテスト |
| 7:00 クイズ ショー | シェークスピア スペシャル (ジェーン・フォンダ) | コメディ アワー (チャーリー・チャップリン) |
| 8:00 サスペンス ドラマ (ソフィア・ローレン) | クラシック アワー (モーツァルト) | スポーツ ニュース |

Make a list of what people want to see. Write personal names and program choices in katakana.

1. Steve (sutiibu): World News.
2. James (jeemusu): Shakespeare Special (with Jane Fonda).
3. Phillip (firippu): Classic Hour (Mozart).
4. Walter (worutaa): Comedy Hour (Charlie Chaplin).
5. Patty (patii): Suspense Drama (with Sophia Loren).
6. Michelle (misheru): Local News.

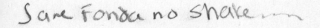

Sane Fonda no shake

# Exercise 2

Your group is planning a year-end get-together. Of the following events, which one do you prefer? Translate the list, and then write your preferences in order in katakana.

a. ファッション　ショー（スキーウェア）
b. ボディービル　コンテスト
c. フォークダンス
d. ディスコ　パーティー
e. チャリティー　コンサート（シンフォニー　オーケストラ）
f. ディナー　ショー（コメディー）

# Appendix: Useful Vocabulary

## Composers

| | | |
|---|---|---|
| 1. バッハ | **ba**hha | Bach |
| 2. ベートーベン | **beetoo**ben | Beethoven |
| 3. ブラームス | bu**raa**musu | Brahms |
| 4. ショパン | **sho**pan | Chopin |
| 5. ドビュッシー | do**byu**sshii | Debussy |
| 6. ハイドン | **hai**don | Haydn |
| 7. リスト | **ri**suto | Liszt |
| 8. メンデルスゾーン | men**derusuzo**on | Mendelssohn |
| 9. モーツァルト | **moo**tsaruto | Mozart |
| 10. シューベルト | **shuu**beruto | Schubert |
| 11. シューマン | **shuu**man | Schumann |
| 12. シュトラウス | shu**tora**usu | Strauss |
| 13. チャイコフスキー | chai**kofusu**kii | Tschaikovsky |
| 14. ワーグナー | **waa**gunaa | Wagner |

## Painters

| | | |
|---|---|---|
| 1. セザンヌ | se**za**nnu | Cézanne |
| 2. シャガール | cha**gaa**ru | Chagall |
| 3. ダ・ビンチ | da**bin**chi | da Vinci |
| 4. ミケランジェロ | mi**ke**ranjero | Michelangelo |
| 5. ミレー | mi**ree** | Millet |
| 6. ミロ | **mi**ro | Miro |
| 7. モネ | **mo**ne | Monet |
| 8. ピカソ | pi**ka**so | Picasso |
| 9. ルノワール | ru**nowa**aru | Renoir |
| 10. ロダン | **ro**dan | Rodin |
| 11. ルソー | **ru**soo | Rousseau |
| 12. ゴッホ | **go**hho | Van Gogh |

## Writers

| | | |
|---|---|---|
| 1. イソップ | **i**soppu | Aesop |
| 2. アンデルセン | **an**derusen | Andersen |
| 3. コクトー | **ko**kutoo | Cocteau |
| 4. ドストエフスキー | do**sutoefu**sukii | Dostoyevski |
| 5. ゲーテ | **gee**te | Goethe |
| 6. グリム | **gu**rimu | Grimm |
| 7. ハイネ | **ha**ine | Heine |

| 8. ヘミングウェー | **hemi**nguwee | Hemingway |
| 9. ヘッセ | **hesse** | Hesse |
| 10. イプセン | **ipu**sen | Ibsen |
| 11. モーパッサン | **moo**passan | Maupassant |
| 12. シェークスピア | shee**kusu**pia | Shakespeare |
| 13. トルストイ | to**rusu**toi | Tolstoy |

## Scientists

| 1. ベル | **be**ru | Bell |
| 2. キューリー | **kyuu**rii | Curie |
| 3. ダーウィン | **daa**win | Darwin |
| 4. エジソン | **e**jison | Edison |
| 5. アインシュタイン | **ain**shutain | Einstein |
| 6. ガリレオ | ga**rireo** | Galileo |
| 7. ニュートン | **nyuu**ton | Newton |
| 8. ノーベル | **noo**beru | Nobel |
| 9. パブロフ | **pa**burofu | Pavlov |
| 10. レントゲン | **ren**togen | Roentgen |
| 11. シュバイツァー | shu**baitsaa** | Schweitzer |

## Brand Names / Fashion Designers

| 1. カルティエ | **ka**rutie | Cartier |
| 2. セリーヌ | se**riinu** | Celine |
| 3. シャネル | **sha**neru | Chanel |
| 4. ディオール | **di**ooru | Dior |
| 5. ダンヒル | **dan**hiru | Dunhill |
| 6. ジバンシィ | ji**ban**shi | Givenchy |
| 7. グッチ | **gu**cchi | Gucci |
| 8. エルメス | **e**rumesu | Hermes |
| 9. ロンジン | **ron**jin | Longines |
| 10. ニナ リッチ | nina**ritchi** | Nina Ricci |
| 11. オメガ | **o**mega | Omega |
| 12. ピアジェ | **pi**aje | Piaget |
| 13. ロレックス | ro**rekku**su | Rolex |
| 14. サンローラン | **san**rooran | Saint Laurent |
| 15. ティファニー | **ti**fanii | Tiffany |

## Hair Salon / Barber

| 1. パーマ※ | **paa**ma | permanent wave, perm |
| 2. カット | **ka**tto | cut |
| 3. ブロー | **bu**roo | blow dry |
| 4. カール | **kaa**ru | curl |
| 5. ロング | **ron**gu | long (hair) |
| 6. ショート | **shoo**to | short (hair) |
| 7. リンス | **rin**su | rinse |
| 8. ムース | **muu**su | mousse [Fr.] |
| 9. カーラー | **kaa**raa | curler |

| | | |
|---|---|---|
| 10. スプレー | supuree | spray |
| 11. シャンプー | shanpuu | shampoo |
| 12. マニキュア | manikyua | nail polish [E., mani-cure] |
| 13. ヘアトニック | heatonikku | hair tonic |
| 14. ヘアスタイル | heasutairu | hairstyle |
| 15. トリートメント | toriitomento | treatment |

## Menu Items

### • Main Courses and Side Dishes

| | | |
|---|---|---|
| 1. パン | pan | bread [Port., pão] |
| 2. ライス | raisu | rice (served on a plate) |
| 3. パスタ | pasuta | pasta |
| 4. ドリア | doria | rice casserole [It., doria] |
| 5. ピラフ | pirafu | pilaf [Fr.] |
| 6. サラダ | sarada | salad |
| 7. シチュー | shichuu | stew |
| 8. グラタン | guratan | casserole [Fr., gratin] |
| 9. オムレツ | omuretsu | omelet [Fr.] |
| 10. ムニエル | munieru | buttered fish [Fr., meunière] |
| 11. ボンゴレ | bongore | white clam sauce (for spaghetti) [It., vongole] |
| 12. コロッケ | korokke | croquette [Fr.] |
| 13. コンソメ | konsome | consommé [Fr.] |
| 14. チャウダー | chaudaa | chowder |
| 15. スパゲティ | supageti | spaghetti [It.] |
| 16. ナポリタン | naporitan | tomato sauce with veg-etables (spaghetti) [It., Napolitain] |
| 17. メンチカツ※ | menchikatsu | hamburger cutlet [E., mince cutlet] |
| 18. オムライス※ | omuraisu | rice omelet |
| 19. ハムサンド※ | hamusando | ham sandwich |
| 20. ハンバーグ※ | hanbaagu | hamburger steak |
| 21. ハンバーガー | hanbaagaa | hamburger (with bun) |
| 22. ミートソース | miitosoosu | meat sauce (for spaghetti) |
| 23. ヒレステーキ | hiresuteeki | filet steak, tenderloin steak |
| 24. ピザトースト | pizatoosuto | pizza sauce and cheese on toast |
| 25. カレーライス | kareeraisu | curry on rice |
| 26. フライドチキン | furaidochikin | fried chicken |
| 27. ミックスサンド※ | mikkususando | mixed (finger) sand-wiches |

| 29. コーンポタージュ | koonpotaaju | corn potage, cream of corn soup |
| 30. ビーフストロガノフ | biifu sutoroganofu | beef stroganoff |

## • Dessert

| 1. パイ | pai | pie |
| 2. パフェ | pafe | parfait, ice cream sundae |
| 3. ケーキ | keeki | cake |
| 4. プリン | purin | (custard) pudding |
| 5. エクレア | ekurea | éclair [Fr.] |
| 6. ババロア | babaroa | Bavarian cream gelatin [Fr., bavarois] |
| 7. シャーベット | shaabetto | sherbet |
| 8. シュークリーム※ | shuukuriimu | cream puff [Fr., chou à la crème] |
| 9. コーヒーゼリー | koohiizerii | coffee-flavored gelatin [E., coffee jelly] |
| 10. アイスクリーム | aisukuriimu | ice cream |

## • Beverages

| 1. ココア | kokoa | cocoa, hot chocolate |
| 2. コーラ | koora | cola |
| 3. ソーダ | sooda | soda [D.] |
| 4. ジュース | juusu | juice |
| 5. コーヒー | koohii | coffee [D., koffie] |
| 6. カフェオレ | kafeore | café au lait [Fr.] |
| 7. アイスティー | aisutii | iced tea |
| 8. レモンティー | remontii | hot tea with lemon [E., lemon tea] |
| 9. ミルクティー | mirukutii | hot tea with milk / cream [E., milk tea] |
| 10. アイスコーヒー | aisukoohii | iced coffee |
| 11. ホットコーヒー | hottokoohii | hot coffee |
| 12. レモンスカッシュ | remon sukasshu | lemon soda [E., lemon squash] |

## • Alcohol

| 1. ラム | ramu | rum |
| 2. ジン | jin | gin |
| 3. ワイン | wain | wine |
| 4. ビール | biiru | beer [D., bier] |
| 5. シェリー | sherii | sherry |
| 6. ウォッカ | wokka | vodka [R.] |
| 7. バーボン | baabon | bourbon |
| 8. テキーラ | tekiira | tequila [Sp.] |
| 9. スコッチ | sukotchi | Scotch |
| 10. カクテル | kakuteru | cocktail |

| | | |
|---|---|---|
| 11. リキュール | ri**kyu**uru | liqueur [Fr.] |
| 12. シャンパン | sha**npan** | champagne [Fr.] |
| 13. ブランデー | bu**randee** | brandy |
| 14. ウイスキー | ui**s**ukii | whiskey |
| 15. ボトル | bo**toru** | bottle (whiskey) |
| 16. グラス | **gu**rasu | glass (whiskey / wine) |
| 17. ジョッキ | **jo**kki | beer mug [E., jug] |
| 18. ダブル | **da**buru | double |
| 19. シングル | **shi**nguru | single |
| 20. オンザロック | o**nzaro**kku | on the rocks |

## Computer Terms

| | | |
|---|---|---|
| 1. ワープロ※ | wa**apuro** | word processor |
| 2. パソコン※ | pa**sokon** | personal computer |
| 3. コンピュータ(ー) | ko**npyuu**ta(a) | computer |
| 4. プリンタ(ー) | pu**rinta(a)** | printer |
| 5. ハードディスク | ha**adodi**suku | hard disk |
| 6. メモリー | **me**morii | memory |
| 7. カーソル | ka**asoru** | cursor |
| 8. フォント | **fo**nto | font |
| 9. シフト | **shi**futo | shift |
| 10. タブ | **ta**bu | tab |
| 11. スペース | su**pee**su | space |
| 12. キーボード | ki**iboo**do | keyboard |
| 13. エラー | e**raa** | error |
| 14. メッセージ | **me**sseeji | message |
| 14. メニュー | **me**nyuu | menu |
| 15. フロッピー※ | fu**roppii** | floppy disk |
| 16. ソフト※ | **so**futo | software |
| 17. ファイル | **fa**iru | file |

# Katakana–English Glossary

アーケード arcade
アーチ arch
アーメン amen
アイオワ Iowa
アイシャドー eye shadow
アイスクリーム ice cream
アイスクリームサンデー ice cream sundae
アイスクリームパフェ ice cream parfait
アイスコーヒー iced coffee
アイススケート ice skating
アイスティー iced tea
アイスホッケー ice hockey
アイダホ Idaho
アイデア idea
アイドル popular teenage singer
アイライン eyeliner
アイルランド Ireland
アイロン iron (for pressing clothes)
アインシュタイン Einstein
アカデミー academy
アクセサリー accessory
アクセル accelerator pedal
アクセント accent
アクリル acrylic
アクロバット acrobat
アコーディオン accordion
アジア Asia
アシスタント assistant
アスパラガス asparagus
アスピリン aspirin
アスファルト asphalt
アダプター (electric power) adapter, AC-DC converter
アップルパイ apple pie
アテネ Athens
アドバイザー adviser
アドバイス advice
アトラクション attraction (program)
アトリエ artist's studio
アドリブ ad-lib
アナウンサー announcer

アナウンス announcement (over a PA system)
アニメ(−ション) animated cartoon
アパート apartment house
アピール appeal (let people know, request)
アフターケア aftercare
アフターサービス after-sales service
アフリカ Africa
アフロヘア Afro hairstyle
アベック dating couple
アマゾン Amazon
アマチュア amateur
アムステルダム Amsterdam
アメリカ America
アラカルト a la carte
アラスカ Alaska
アラビア Arabia
アラブ Arab
アリゾナ Arizona
アリバイ alibi
アルカリ alkali
アルコール alcohol
アルゼンチン Argentina
アルバイト side job
アルバム album
アルファベット alphabet
アルプス the Alps
アルミ(ニウム) aluminum
アレルギー allergy
アンケート questionnaire
アンコール encore
アンサンブル ensemble
アンチョビ anchovy
アンデス Andes
アンテナ antenna
アンデルセン Andersen
アンバランス imbalance, unbalanced
アンプ amplifier, amp
アンモニア ammonia

イースター Easter
イースト yeast
イオン ion
イギリス United Kingdom
イクラ salted salmon roe
イスラエル Israel
イソップ Aesop
イタリア Italy
イニシャル (one's) initials
イプセン Ibsen
イベント program of entertainments
イミテーション imitation
イメージ image
イメージチェンジ change one's image
イヤホーン earphone
イヤリング earring
イラク Iraq
イラスト illustration
イラストレーター illustrator
イラン Iran
イリノイ Illinois
イルミネーション illumination
インク ink
インスタント instant
インスタントコーヒー instant coffee
インターナショナル international
インターハイ inter high school athletic
  competition
インターン intern
インタビュー interview
インタホン interphone, intercom
インチ inch
インディアン (American) Indian
インテリ intellectual
インテリア interior decorations
イントネーション intonation
インドネシア Indonesia
イントロ introduction (musical)
インフォーマル informal
インフォメーション information (desk)
インフルエンザ influenza
インフレ inflation

ウーマンリブ women's lib
ウール wool
ウィーン Vienna
ウイスキー whiskey
ウイルス virus
ウインカー blinker

ウインク wink
ウエーター waiter
ウエートレス waitress
ウエスタン western (movie, music)
ウエスト waist
ウェディングケーキ wedding cake
ウェディングドレス wedding dress
ウエハース wafer
ウォークマン Walkman
ウォッカ vodka
ウォルター Walter
ウクレレ ukulele

エープリルフール April Fools' day
エアコン air conditioner
エアメール airmail
エアロビクス aerobics
エキストラ extra (in a movie)
エクレア éclair
エゴイスト egoist, egotist
エコノミークラス economy class (on
  planes)
エジソン Edison
エジプト Egypt
エスカレーター escalator
エスキモー Eskimo
エチケット etiquette
エナメル enamel
エネルギー energy
エピソード episode
エプロン apron
エラー (computer, baseball) error
エリート elite (person)
エルサレム Jerusalem
エルメス Hermes
エレガント elegant
エレベーター elevator
エンゲージリング engagement ring
エンジニア engineer
エンジン engine
エンジンキー ignition key
エンスト stalled engine

オークション auction
オーケストラ orchestra
オーストラリア Australia
オーダーストップ last order (food /
  drinks)
オーダーメード custom made

オーディオ　audio
オーディション　audition (test)
オーデコロン　cologne
オートバイ　motorcycle
オードブル　hors d'oeuvre
オートミール　oatmeal
オートメーション　automation
オートレース　auto race
オートロック　automatic locking door
オーナー　owner
オーバー　overcoat, overdone
　(exaggeration)
オーブン　oven
オープンカー　open convertible (car)
オーブントースター　toaster oven
オールナイト　all-night
オーロラ　aurora
オアシス　oasis
オイル　oil
オイルチェンジ　oil change
オカルト　occult
オクターブ　octave
オクラ　okra
オクラホマ　Oklahoma
オセロ　Othello
オパール　opal
オペラ　opera
オペラグラス　opera glasses
オペレーター　(telephone) operator
オホーツク　Okhotsk
オムライス　rice omelette
オムレツ　omelette
オメガ　Omega
オランダ　Holland
オリーブ　olive
オリジナル　original
オリンピック　the Olympics
オルガン　(reed) organ
オルゴール　music box
オレンジ　orange (color, fruit)
オンザロック　on the rocks
オンス　ounce

ガーゼ　gauze
カーソル　cursor
カーテン　curtain
カード　card (not playing cards)
ガード　guard; railroad trestle
ガードマン　security guard, watchman

カーネーション　carnation
カーブ　curve
カーペット　carpet
カーボン　carbon (paper)
カーラー　curler
カール　curl; Carl
ガールスカウト　Girl Scout=the Girl
　Scouts
ガールフレンド　girl friend
ガイド　a guide
カイロ　Cairo
カウンセラー　counselor
カウンセリング　counseling
カウンター　counter
カクテル　cocktail
カシミア　cashmere
ガス　gas
カセットテープ　cassette tape
ガソリン　gasoline
ガソリンスタンド　gas station, service
　station
カタログ　catalog
カット　cut
カップ　coffee cup, trophy cup
カップル　(male & female) couple
カトリック　Catholic
カナリア　canary
カヌー　canoe
カバー　cover, covering
カフェイン　caffeine
カフェオレ　café au lait
カフス　cuff, cuff link
カプセル　capsule
カプセルホテル　inexpensive hotel with
　capsule-shaped sleeping compartments
ガム　(chewing) gum
ガムテープ　masking tape
カメオ　cameo
カメラ　camera
カメラアングル　camera angle
カメラマン　cameraman, photographer
カメレオン　chameleon
カラー　color (TV, photo)
ガラス　glass (the material)
カリフォルニア　California
カリフラワー　cauliflower
ガリレオ　Galileo
カルシウム　calcium
カルチャーショック　culture shock

カルテ patient's hospital chart
カルティエ Cartier
カレーライス curry on rice
カレンダー calendar
カロリー calorie
カンガルー kangaroo
カンニング cheating on a written test
カンパ fund raising campaign/collection

キーボード key board
キーホルダー key chain
キウイ kiwi
キス kiss
ギター guitar
ギブス plaster cast
ギフト gift
ギャグ a gag (joke)
キャスト cast (of a play)
キャッシュカード cash card
キャッチフレーズ catchword (slogan)
キャッチボール the game of "catch"
キャディー (golf) caddie
キャビア caviar
キャプテン captain
キャラメル caramel
ギャラリー (art) gallery, spectators
キャリア career experience
ギャング gangster
キャンセル cancel, cancellation
キャンパス (usually college) campus
キャンプ camp
キャンプファイア campfire
ギャンブル gamble, gambling
キャンペーン campaign
キューリー Curie
キュロット culottes
ギリシャ Greece
キリスト Christ
キロ kilometer
キログラム kilogram
キロメートル kilometer

クーデター coup d'état
クーポン coupon
クーラー air conditioner, ice chest
クイズ quiz
クッキー cookie
クッション cushion
グッチ Gucci

グッピー guppy
グラ(ウ)ンド the grounds
グライダー glider (plane)
クライマックス climax
クラクション (car) horn
クラシック classical music
クラス class
グラス liquor (beer, whiskey, wine), glass
クラスメート classmate
グラタン casserole
クラッカー (soda) cracker
クラブ club(group), club(playing cards)
グラフ graph
クリーニング dry cleaning
クリーム cream
クリス Chris
クリスマス Christmas
クリスマスイブ Christmas Eve
クリスマスツリー Christmas tree
クリップ (paper/hair) clip
グリム Grimm
グリル grill
クルーザー (cabin) cruiser
グループ group
グルメ gourmet
クレープ crepe
グレープフルーツ grapefruit
クレーム complaint (for damages, etc.)
クレーン crane (machine)
クレジット credit (payment)
クレジットカード credit card
クレソン watercress
クレヨン crayon
クレンザー cleanser
クローク cloakroom
クローバー clover
グローブ (boxing, baseball) glove
クロール crawl (swimming stroke)
グロテスク grotesque
クロワッサン croissant

ケーキ cake
ケース case
ゲーテ Goethe
ゲート (airport, horse race starting) gate
ケーブルカー cable car
ゲーム game (other than sports)
ゲームセンター video arcade

ゲスト guest
ケチャップ ketchup
ケニア Kenya
ゲリラ guerrilla
ケルン Cologne (Köln)
ゲレンデ ski slope

ゴーグル goggles
コースター coaster
コーチ coach
コード cord, chord, code
コードレス cordless
コーナー special counter or section
コーヒー coffee
コーヒーゼリー coffee-flavored gelatin
コーラ cola
コーラス chorus
ゴールデン アワー prime time
ゴールデンウィーク Golden Week
  holidays (Apr. 29–May 5)
コーン corn; (ice cream) cone
コーンスターチ cornstarch
コーンフレーク cornflakes
コーンポタージュ corn potage, cream
  of corn soup
コアラ koala
コインランドリー Laundromat,
  launderette
コインロッカー coin-operated locker
コカコーラ Coca Cola
コクトー Cocteau
ココア cocoa, hot chocolate
ゴシップ gossip
コック cook, chef
コップ (drinking/water) glass
ゴッホ Van Gogh
コピー copy (usually photocopy)
コピーライター copywriter
コブラ cobra
コマーシャル commercial
コミュニケーション communication
コミュニティー community
ゴム rubber
コメディアン comedian
コメント comment
ゴリラ gorilla
コルク cork
ゴルフ golf
コレクトコール collect call

コレステロール cholesterol
コレラ cholera
コロッケ croquette
コロンブス Columbus
コンクリート concrete (cement)
コンサート concert
コンサートホール concert hall
コンサルタント consultant
コンセント wall outlet, wall socket
コンソメ consommé
コンタクトレンズ contact lens
コンディション (one's body) condition
コンテスト contest
コントロール control
コンパ college students' party
コンパクト compact
コンパス compasses
コンビ a duo, matched-up pair (people)
コンビニ(エンス ストア) convenience
  store
コンピュータ(ー) computer
コンプレックス inferiority complex
コンペ (golf) tournament
コンベヤーベルト conveyor belt

サーカス circus
サークル circle (group with common
  interest)
サーチライト searchlight
サービス service, discount price, free
  of charge
サーブ serve (ball)
サーファー surfer
サーフィング surfing
サーフボード surfboard
サーロインステーキ sirloin steak
サイクリング cycling
サイズ size
サイドブレーキ hand/parking brake
サイレン siren
サイロ silo
サイン signature, autograph, signal
サインペン felt pen
サウナ sauna
サッカー soccer
サテン satin
サファイア sapphire
サファリパーク safari park
サボテン cactus

108

サマースクール　summer school
サモア　Samoa
サラダ　salad
サラミ　salami
サラリーマン　male white-collar worker
サロン　salon
サワークリーム　sour cream
サングラス　sunglasses
サンタクロース　Santa Claus
サンダル　sandal(s)
サンドイッチ　sandwich
サンバ　samba
サンフランシスコ　San Francisco
サンプル　sample (product)
サンローラン　Saint Laurent

シーズン　season
シーズン・オフ　off-season
シーソー　seesaw
シーツ　(bed) sheet(s)
シートベルト　seat belt
ジーパン　jeans
ジープ　jeep
シール　sticker
シーン　scene
ジーンズ　jeans
シアトル　Seattle
シェークスピア　Shakespeare
ジェットコースター　roller coaster
シェフ　chef
シェリー　sherry
シカゴ　Chicago
ジグザグ　zigzag
システム　system
シチュー　stew
シドニー　Sydney
シナモン　cinnamon
シナリオ　scenario
シネマ　cinema
ジバンシィ　Givenchy
シフト　(keyboard) shift
シベリア　Siberia
ジャージー　sweat pants/suit
ジャーナリスト　journalist
シャープペン(シル)　mechanical pencil
シャーベット　sherbet
シャガール　Chagall
ジャケット　jacket
ジャズ　jazz

シャツ　undershirt, shirt
シャッター　shutter (door, camera)
シャネル　Chanel
シャベル　shovel
ジャム　(fruit) jam
シャワー　shower
ジャングル　jungle
シャンソン　chanson
シャンデリア　chandelier
ジャンパー　jacket (casual)
ジャンパースカート　jumper (dress)
シャンパン　champagne
シャンプー　shampoo
ジャンル　genre
ジュークボックス　jukebox
シュークリーム　cream puff
ジュース　juice
シューベルト　Schubert
シューマン　Schumann
シュトラウス　Strauss
シュバイツァー　Schweitzer
ジョージ　George
ショート　short (hair)
ショートケーキ　(usually strawberry)
　shortcake
ショールーム　showroom
ジョギング　jogging
ジョッキ　beer mug
ショッピング　shopping
ショパン　Chopin
シリーズ　series
シリアル　cereal
シルク　silk
シルバーシート　"silver seat" (seats on
　buses and trains reserved for the
　elderly)
ジレンマ　dilemma
シロップ　(maple, sugar)syrup
ジン　gin
ジンクス　jinx, superstition
シングル　single
シングルス　(tennis) singles
シンクロ(ナイズドスイミング)
　synchronized swimming
シンセサイザー　synthesizer
シンフォニー　symphony
シンポジウム　symposium
シンボル　symbol

スー Sue
スーツ (business) suit
スーツケース suitcase
スーパー supermarket; movie subtitle
スーパーマン superman
スープ soup
ズームレンズ zoom lens
スイス Switzerland
スイッチ (electric) switch
スウェーデン Sweden
スカート skirt
スカーフ scarf
スカンク skunk
スキー ski(s), skiing
スキーウェア skiwear
スキーリフト ski lift
スキャンダル scandal
スクーター scooter
スクープ scoop (news)
スクリーン (movie) screen
スケート (ice) skating
スケール scale
スケジュール schedule
スコア score
スコッチ Scotch
スコップ shovel
スター star (performer)
スタート start
スタートライン starting line
スタイリスト fashion stylist
スタイル (fashion) style; one's figure
スタジアム stadium
スタジオ studio (not apartment)
スタミナ stamina
スタンド bleachers, desk / floor lamp
スタントマン stunt man
スタンプ rubber stamp
スチームアイロン steam iron
スチュワーデス stewardess
ステーキ steak
ステージ stage
ステッキ (walking) stick, cane
ステレオ stereo
ステンドグラス stained glass
ステンレス stainless steel
スト (labor) strike
ストーブ heater
ストッキング nylon stockings
ストック ski poles

ストップウォッチ stopwatch
ストライキ (labor) strike
ストライク (baseball, bowling) strike
ストレート straight (game score, whiskey)
ストレス (psychological) stress
ストロー straw (for drinking)
スナック bar
スニーカー sneaker
スノーケル snorkel
スノータイヤ snow tire
スパイ spy
スパゲティ spaghetti
スピーカー (audio) speaker
スピーチ speech
スピード speed
スプーン spoon
スプレー spray
スペース (typing) space
スペード spade (playing cards)
スペイン Spain
スポーツ sport
スポーツカー sports car
スポーツマン sportsman
スポットライト spotlight
ズボン trousers, pants
スポンサー sponsor
スポンジ sponge
スマート smart (i.e., stylish, slender)
スモッグ smog
スライド a slide (photography)
スラム slum
スリッパ (indoor) slippers
スリル thrill
スローガン slogan
スローモーション slow motion

セーター sweater
セーヌ Seine
セーフ safe (baseball)
セール (bargain) sale
セクハラ sexual harassment
セザンヌ Cézanne
セスナ Cessna (plane)
ゼッケン athlete's shirt number
セミナー seminar
セメント cement
ゼラチン gelatin (substance)
ゼリー gelatin dessert

110

セリーヌ　Celine
セルフサービス　self-service
ゼロ　zero
セロテープ　adhesive cellophane tape
セロハン　cellophane
セロリ　celery
センサー　sensor
センターライン　center line
センチ(メートル)　centimeter
センチメンタル　sentimental
セント　cent

ソース　sauce (usually Worcestershire)
ソーセージ　sausage
ソーダ　carbonated drink, soda
ゾーン　zone
ソウル　Seoul, soul music
ソックス　sock(s)
ソテー　sauté
ソニー　Sony
ソビエト　the Soviet Union
ソファー　sofa
ソフト　software; soft
ソフトクリーム　soft ice cream
ソプラノ　soprano
ソロ　solo (music)

ダ・ビンチ　da Vinci
ダーウィン　Darwin
ターザン　tarzan
タートルネック　turtleneck
ターミナル　(airport, bus) terminal
タイ　Thailand
ダイエット　(weight control) diet
ダイナマイト　dynamite
ダイニング　dining room
ダイニングキッチン　dinette
ダイビング　diving
タイプ　type
タイプライター　typewriter
タイマー　timer
タイミング　timing
タイム　time; thyme
タイムアウト　timeout
ダイヤ　diamond; train or plane
　timetable
タイヤ　tire
ダイヤ（モンド）　diamond
ダイヤル　dial

タイル　tile
タウンページ　yellow pages
タオル　towel
タキシード　tuxedo
タクシー　taxi
タクト　conductor's baton
タバコ　cigarette
タバスコ　Tabasco
タヒチ　Tahiti
ダビング　(film, tape) dubbing
タフ　tough, healthy, sturdy (person)
タブ　(typing) tab
タブー　taboo
ダブル　double
ダム　dam
タレント　TV personality
タワー　tower
タンカー　tanker
タンク　tank
タンゴ　tango
ダンサー　dancer
ダンス　dance
ダンヒル　Dunhill
ダンプカー　dump truck

チーズ　cheese
チーズケーキ　cheesecake
チーム　team
チームワーク　teamwork
チェーン　chain
チェス　chess
チェックアウト　checkout
チェックイン　check-in
チェックポイント　check point
チェロ　cello
チップ　tip(gratuity), chip(s)
チャーター　charter (planes, etc.)
チャーミング　charming
チャームポイント　charm point
チャイコフスキー　Tschaikovsky
チャイム　chime
チャウダー　chowder
チャック　zipper (trousers)
チャリティーショー　charity show
チャレンジ　challenge
チャンス　chance, opportunity
チャンネル　(TV) channel
チャンピオン　champion
チューブ　tube

チョーク chalk
チョコレート chocolate
チョッキ vest
チリ Chile

ツアー tour
ツイン twin (bed)
ツナ (canned) tuna

データ data
デート date (boy-girl)
テープ tape
テーブル table (furniture)
テープレコーダー tape recorder
テーマ theme
ティーシャツ T-shirt
ディーゼル diesel
ディオール Dior
ディスコ disco
ディズニーランド Disneyland
ティッシュ(ペーパー) tissue paper
ティファニー Tiffany
ディレクター director
テキーラ tequila
テキサス Texas
テキスト textbook
テクニック technique
テクノロジー technology
デザート dessert
デザイナー designer
デザイン design
デジタル digital
テスト test
デッサン a sketch (drawing)
テニス tennis
テニスコート tennis court
デニム denim
テネシー Tennessee
デパート department store
デビュー debut
デマ false rumor
デモ demonstration (protest)
デュエット duet
テラス terrace
デラックス deluxe
デリケート delicate
テレパシー telepathy
テレビ television
テロ terrorism

テント tent
テンポ tempo

ドア door
トースター toaster
トースト toast (bread)
ドーナツ doughnut
トーナメント tournament
トーマス Thomas
ドーム dome
ドイツ Germany
トイレ toilet, restroom
トイレットペーパー toilet paper
ドキュメンタリー documentary (film)
ドストエフスキー Dostoyevski
トピック topic
ドビュッシー Debussy
トマト tomato
ドミノ domino
トム Tom
ドライアイス dry ice
ドライブ driving for pleasure
ドライヤー hair dryer
ドラキュラ Dracula, vampire
トラクター tractor
トラック truck; track
ドラマ (TV, radio) drama
ドラム drum
トランク (car) trunk
トランクルーム storage room
トランプ playing cards
トランペット trumpet
トランポリン trampoline
トリートメント treatment (for hair)
ドリア rice casserole
トリオ trio
ドル dollar
トルストイ Tolstoy
トレードマーク trademark
トレーナー sweat shirt
トレーニング training
トレーラー trailer
ドレス a dress
ドレッシング (salad) dressing
トロピカル tropical
トロフィー trophy
トン ton
トンネル tunnel

112

ナイーブ naive
ナイアガラ Niagara
ナイター night game (usually baseball)
ナイフ knife
ナイル Nile
ナイロン nylon
ナッツ nut
ナプキン napkin
ナフタリン naphthalene, mothball
ナポリタン tomato sauce with
　vegetables (spaghetti)
ナポレオン Napoleon
ナレーション narration
ナレーター narrator
ナンシー Nancy
ナンセンス nonsense

ニース Nice
ニクソン Nixon
ニコチン nicotine
ニス varnish
ニックネーム nickname
ニット knitwear
ニナ　リッチ Nina Ricci
ニュースキャスター newscaster
ニュートン Newton
ニューヨーク New York
ニュアンス nuance

ヌード nude

ネオン neon
ネガ (film) negative
ネクター thick fruit beverage
ネクタイ necktie
ネクタイピン tiepin, tie tack
ネックレス necklace
ネットワーク network
ネル flannel

ノーコメント no comment
ノート notebook
ノーベル Nobel
ノーマル normal
ノイローゼ neurosis, nervous
　breakdown
ノック knock (on a door)
ノックアウト knockout
ノミネート nominate

ノルウェー Norway
ノルマ norm, (assigned) production
　quota

バー (saloon) bar
バーゲン bargain (sale)
バーコード bar code
パーセント percent
パーティー party
バーテン（ダー）bartender
ハート hearts (playing cards)
パート(タイム) part-time
ハードディスク hard disk
パートナー partner
ハードル hurdle
ハープ harp
ハーフタイム half time
バーベキュー barbecue
バーベル barbell
バーボン bourbon
パーマ permanent wave, perm
ハーモニカ harmonica
パイ pie
バイオリン violin
ハイカー hiker
ハイキング hiking
バイキング buffet
バイク motorbike, motorcycle
ハイジャック hijacking
バイタリティー vitality
ハイテク advanced technology
バイト side job
ハイドン Haydn
パイナップル pineapple
ハイネ Heine
ハイヒール high-heeled shoes
パイプ pipe
ハイファイ Hi-Fi
ハイフン hyphen
ハイヤー hired taxi
ハイライト highlight
バイリンガル bilingual
パイロット (aircraft) pilot
バクテリア bacteria
バケツ bucket, pail
バザー bazaar
パジャマ pajamas
バス bus; bath; bass (vocal part)
パス pass

113

パスタ pasta
バスタオル bath towel
バスト women's bust (not statue)
パスポート passport
パズル puzzle
パセリ parsley
パソコン personal computer
バター butter
バックミラー rear-view mirror
バッジ badge
バッハ Bach
パトカー (police) patrol car
パトロール patrol
バナナ banana
パニック panic
ハネムーン honeymoon
パネル panel
パノラマ panorama
パパ papa
ババロア Bavarian cream gelatin
パブ pub
パフェ parfait, ice cream sundae
ハプニング an unexpected occurrence
パブロフ Pavlov
ハム ham
ハムサンド ham sandwich
バラード ballade
パラシュート parachute
バランス balance
パリ Paris
バリケード barricade
ハリケーン hurricane
バルコニー balcony
パルプ pulp(wood)
パレード parade
バレー(ボール) volleyball
バレエ ballet
バレリーナ ballerina
ハレルヤ hallelujah
バレンタインデー Valentine's Day
ハロウィーン Halloween
バロック baroque
パロディー parody
バロメーター barometer
ハワイ Hawaii
パン bread
ハンガー hanger
ハンガーストライキ hunger strike
ハンカチ handkerchief

パンク flat tire, over full capacity,
  punk (rock)
ハンサム handsome man
ハンスト hunger strike
パンスト panty hose
パンダ panda
パンツ underpants
バンド (music) band, (watch) band
(ハンド)バッグ handbag, purse
パントマイム pantomime
ハンドル handlebars, steering wheel
ハンバーガー hamburger (with bun)
ハンバーグ hamburger steak
パンプス pumps (shoes)
パンフレット pamphlet, brochure
ハンマー hammer
ハンモック hammock

ビーズ (handicraft) bead(s)
ビーカー beaker
ピーク peak
ヒーター heater
ビーチタオル beach towel
ビートルズ The Beatles
ピーナッツ peanut
ピーナッツバター peanut butter
ビーフストロガノフ beef stroganoff
ピーマン green pepper
ヒール (shoe) heel
ビール beer
ビールス virus
ビアガーテン beer garden
ピアジェ Piaget
ピアス pierced earrings
ピアニスト pianist
ピアノ piano
ピエロ clown
ピカソ Picasso
ビキニ bikini
ピクニック picnic
ピザ pizza
ビザ visa
ピザトースト pizza sauce and cheese
  on toast
ビジネスホテル inexpensive hotels
  mainly used on business trips
ビジネスマン businessman
ビスケット biscuit, (sweet) cracker
ヒステリー hysteria

114

ピストル pistol
ビタミン vitamin
ヒッチハイク hitchhike
ヒットチャート hit chart (music)
ヒップ hip(s), hipline
ビデオ video
ビデオデッキ video deck
ビニール vinyl, plastic (bag)
ビニールハウス plastic greenhouse
ヒマラヤ Himalaya
ヒューズ fuse
ピラフ pilaf
ピラミッド pyramid
ビリヤード billiards, pool
ビル concrete building, Bill
ヒレ filet
ヒレステーキ filet steak, tenderloin
　steak
ビロード velvet
ピンセット tweezers
ピント focus (camera)
ヒント hint
ピンポン ping pong

ブーケ bouquet
ブーツ boots
ブーム boom, fad
プール (swimming) pool
ファーストクラス first class (plane &
　boat seats)
ファーストフード fast-food
ファイト fighting spirit, fervor
ファイバーグラス fiber glass
ファイバースコープ fiberscope
ファイル file (papers)
ファインダー (view) finder
ファクシミリ facsimile
ファスナー zipper
ファ(ッ)クス fax
ファッション fashion
ファミリーレストラン family
　restaurant/diner
ファン fan (admirer)
ファンタジー fantasy
ファンヒーター fan heater
ファンファーレ fanfare
ブイ buoy
フィート foot / feet (measurement)
フィアンセ fiancé , fiancée

フィクション fiction
フィットネス fitness
フィナーレ finale (stage show)
フィリピン the Philippines
フィルター filter
フィルハーモニー philharmony
フィルム film (roll)
フェアプレー fair play
フェミニスト gallant man, feminist
フェリー ferry
フェルト felt (cloth)
フェンシング fencing (sport)
フォーク fork; folk music
フォークソング folk song
フォークダンス folk dance
フォーマル formal
フォント font
ブザー buzzer
プッシュホン push button phone
フットボール football
ブティック boutique
ブラームス Brahms
フライ fly (baseball); fry
フライト (airplane) flight
プライド pride
フライドチキン fried chicken
フライドポテト french fries
プライバシー privacy
フライパン frying pan
プライベート private
ブラインド (Venetian) blinds
ブラウス blouse
プラカード placard
プラグ (electric) plug
ブラシ brush
ブラジル Brazil
プラス plus
プラスアルファ something plus a little
　more
プラスチック plastic
ブラスバンド brass band
プラチナ platinum
ブラックリスト blacklist
フラッシュ flash (photography)
プラネタリウム planetarium
フラミンゴ flamingo
フラメンコ flamenco
プラモデル plastic model (toys)
プラン plan

ブランク blank (period)
プランクトン plankton
フランクフルト Frankfurt
ブランコ swing
フランス France
フランスパン French bread
ブランデー brandy
ブランド reputable brand name (usually for expensive designer goods)
フリーサイズ one size fits all
フリーダイヤル toll free call
プリーツ pleats
フリーパス free pass
ブリキ tinplate
フリズビー frisbee
プリズム prism
フリル frill
プリン (custard) pudding
プリンタ(ー) (computer) printer
ブルース blues
フルーツ fruit
フルート flute
フルコース full-course
フルタイム full time
ブレーキ brake (cars, bicycles, etc)
フレーム (bowling, eyeglass) frame
フレアスカート flared skirt
プレイガイド theater ticket agency
ブレスレット bracelet
プレゼント present (gift)
プレタポルテ (expensive) ready-made dress
プレッシャー pressure (psychological)
プレハブ prefabricated structure
プレミア(ム) premium
プロ professional; (movie) production
ブロー blow dry
ブローカー broker
ブローチ brooch
フローリング wooden floor
プログラマー (computer) programmer
プログラム program
プロジェクト a project
プロセスチーズ process cheese
プロダクション (film) production
ブロック (cement) block
ブロッコリー broccoli
フロッピー floppy (disk)

プロデューサー producer
プロパンガス propane gas
プロフィール profile (biographical sketch)
プロペラ propeller
プロポーズ marriage proposal
ブロマイド movie star and singer's still picture
プロレス professional wrestling
フロント front desk (in hotel)
フロントガラス windshield

ベーコン bacon
ページ page
ベージュ beige
ベートーベン Beethoven
ペーパータオル paper towel
ペーパードライバー driver on paper only, licensed non-driver
ベール veil
ペア pair (two people)
ヘアクリーム hair cream
ヘアスタイル hairstyle
ヘアトニック hair tonic
ヘアピース hairpiece
ヘアピン hairpin
ヘクタール hectare
ベスト vest, best
ベストセラー best seller
ペダル pedal
ヘッセ Hesse
ベッド bed
ペット pet (animal)
ベッドタウン bedroom community, suburbs
ペットフード pet food
ヘッドホン headphone
ベテラン veteran (expert)
ベトナム Vietnam
ペニシリン penicillin
ベニヤ veneer, plywood
ペパーミント peppermint
ベビーカー stroller
ベビーシッター baby-sitter
ヘビースモーカー heavy smoker
ベビーブーム baby boom
ベビーベッド crib
ヘミングウェー Hemingway
ベランダ veranda

116

ペリカン pelican
ヘリコプター helicopter
ベル Bell
ベルギー Belgium
ヘルスメーター bathroom scale
ヘルツ Hertz
ベルト belt
ヘルニア hernia
ベルベット velvet
ヘルメット helmet
ベルリン Berlin
ヘレン ケラー Helen Keller
ペンキ house paint
ペンギン penguin
ベンジン benzine
ペンダント pendant
ベンチ bench
ペンチ pinchers, pliers
ベンツ Mercedes-Benz
ペンネーム pen name
ペンパル pen pal
ヘンリー Henry

ボーイスカウト Boy Scouts
ボーイフレンド boy friend
ポーカー poker
ポーカーフェース poker face
ボーカル vocal (music)
ホース (water) hose
ポーズ pose, pause
ポーター porter
ポータブル portable
ボート boat, rowboat
ボーナス bonus
ホーム (train) platform; home plate
ホームシック homesickness
ホームラン home run
ホームルーム homeroom
ボールペン ballpoint pen
ボイコット boycott
ボイラー boiler
ホイル (aluminum) foil
ボウリング bowling
ボクサー boxer
ボクシング boxing
ポケット pocket
ポケットベル、ポケベル pager, beeper
ポスター poster
ホステス (bar) hostess

ホスト host
ポスト post (position); mail box (on
  street corner)
ボストン Boston
ボストンバッグ Boston bag, overnight
  bag
ポタージュ potage (soup)
ボタン button
ホック (garment) hook
ホッチキス stapler
ポット thermos bottle
ホットケーキ hotcake, pancake
ホットコーヒー hot coffee
ポップコーン popcorn
ポップス pop music
ボディーガード body guard
ボディーチェック body search / frisk
ボディービル body-building
ポテトチップ potato chip(s)
ホテル hotel
ボトル (whiskey) bottle
ホノルル Honolulu
ポピュラー popular (music)
ポラロイド Polaroid
ボランティア volunteer
ポリエステル polyester
ボリューム volume (sound, amount)
ボルト bolt, volt
ホルモン hormone
ポロシャツ polo shirt
ホワイトハウス the White House
ホワイトボード white board
ボンゴレ white clam sauce (for
  spaghetti)
ボンネット hood
ポンプ pump

マーガリン margarine
マーク Mark (name); a mark
マーケティング marketing
マーチ march
マイアミ Miami
マイカー privately owned car
マイク Mike; microphone
マイコン microcomputer
マイナス minus
マイペース at one's own pace
マイホーム privately owned home
マイル mile

マカオ Macao
マカロニ macaroni
マクドナルド McDonald's
マジックペン magic marker
マスカラ mascara
マスク mask (gauze, respirator)
マスコット mascot
マスコミ mass media
マスタード mustard
マスト mast
マッサージ massage
マッシュルーム mushroom
マッチ match (for fire)
マットレス mattress
マトン mutton
マナー manners (etiquette)
マニア fanatic (e.g., car freak)
マニキュア nail polish
マニュアル manual (handbook)
マニラ Manila
マネージャー (store) manager
マネキン mannequin
マフラー muffler; winter scarf
ママ mamma, mom; female bar
  manager
ママレード marmalade
マヨネーズ mayonnaise
マラソン marathon
マルク German mark
マルクス Marx
マレーシア Malaysia
マロン chestnut
マンション condominium
マンツーマン one-on-one
マント mantle, cloak, cape
マンホール manhole
マンモス mammoth

ミートソース meat sauce (for
  spaghetti)
ミイラ mummy
ミキサー blender; concrete mixer
ミケランジェロ Michelangelo
ミサイル missile
ミシガン Michigan
ミシン sewing machine
ミス mistake; Miss
ミステリー mystery
ミスプリント misprint

ミスユニバース Miss Universe
ミセス Mrs.
ミックスサンド mixed (finger)
  sandwiches
ミッションスクール mission school
ミニスカート miniskirt
ミニチュア miniature
ミネソタ Minnesota
ミネラル mineral
ミネラルウォーター mineral water
ミュージカル musical (play)
ミラノ Milano
ミリメートル millimeter
ミルク milk, coffee cream
ミルクティー hot tea with milk / cream
ミレー Millet
ミロ Miro
ミンク mink
ミント mint

ムース mousse (dessert, hair cream)
ムード atmosphere, ambience
ムームー muumuu
ムニエル buttered fish

メーカー manufacturer
メーター meter (gauge)
メーデー May Day
メートル meter
メアリー Mary
メイク make-up (cosmetics)
メガホン megaphone
メキシコ Mexico
メス surgical knife
メダル medal
メタル metal
メッセージ message
メドレー medley
メトロノーム metronome
メニュー menu
メモ memo
メモリー memory (computer)
メリー Mary
メリークリスマス Merry Christmas
メリット merit
メロディー melody
メロン melon
メンチカツ hamburger cutlet
メンデルスゾーン Mendelssohn

118

メンバー member

モーター motor
モーツァルト Mozart
モーパッサン Maupassant
モカ mocha (coffee)
モスクワ Moscow
モットー motto
モデル model
モナコ Monaco
モニター (TV) monitor, consumer tester
モネ Monet
モノクロ monochrome
モノレール monorail
モヘア mohair
モルモット guinea pig
モントリオール Montreal

ヤマハ Yamaha

ユースホステル youth hostel
ユーターン U-turn
ユーモア humor
ユーモラス humorous
ユーラシア Eurasia
ユタ Utah
ユダヤ Judea, Jewish
ユニーク unique
ユニセフ UNICEF
ユニホーム (sport) uniform
ユネスコ UNESCO

ヨーグルト yogurt
ヨーヨー yo-yo
ヨーロッパ Europe
ヨガ yoga
ヨット yacht, sailboat

ラーメン ramen (Chinese noodles in hot soup)
ライオン lion
ライス cooked rice (served on a plate)
ライター (cigarette) lighter
ライト (stage, car) light(s); lightweight class (boxing)
ライバル rival
ライブ live music
ライフル rifle

ライフワーク lifework
ライム lime
ラウンジ lounge
ラオス Laos
ラグビー rugby
ラケット (tennis) racket, (Ping-Pong) paddle
ラジオ radio
ラジカセ radio cassette player
ラジコン radio control (toy / models)
ラストオーダー last order (food / drinks)
ラスベガス Las Vegas
ラッシュアワー rush hour
ラップ (plastic) wrap
ラフ casual attire
ラブレター love letter
ラベル label
ラミネート lamination
ラム rum; lamb (meat)
ラリー Larry; (car) rally
ランチ lunch
ランドセル (elementary school student's) hard leather knapsack
ランナー runner
ランプ freeway on/off ramp; oil/kerosene lamp

リーグ (baseball) league
リーダー leader
リーダーシップ leadership
リード lead, (instrument) reed
リキュール liqueur
リクエスト request (usually songs)
リクライニングシート reclining seat
リクルート recruit
リサイクル recycle
リサイタル recital
リスク risk
リスト list; Liszt
リズム rhythm
リゾート resort
リハーサル rehearsal
リバイバル revival
リハビリ rehabilitation
リビング living room
リフォーム major alterations to clothing or a home
リフト (ski) lift

リベート rebate
リポート a report
リボン ribbon
リマ Lima
リムジン limousine
リモコン remote control
リューマチ rheumatism
リラ lira
リラックス relax
リレー relay (race)
リンク rink
リンス rinse (for hair)

ルージュ rouge
ルーマニア Romania
ルームメート roommate
ルール rule
ルーレット roulette
ルソー Rousseau
ルノワール Renoir
ルビー ruby

レーザー laser
レーサー racer
レーザーディスク laser disc
レース race; lace
レーズン raisin
レーダー radar
レート rate (of exchange)
レーヨン rayon
レール rail
レイアウト layout
レインコート rain coat
レオタード leotard(s)
レギュラー regular (member)
レコード (music) record
レジ cash register
レシート receipt (cash register)
レシーバー (electric wave) receiver
レジャー leisure time amusement,
  recreation
レストラン restaurant
レスラー wrestler
レスリング wrestling
レタス lettuce
レディーファースト ladies first
レバー liver, lever
レパートリー repertory
レビュー revue

レベル level
レポート a report
レモン lemon
レモンスカッシュ lemon soda
レモンティー hot tea with lemon
レンジ kitchen range (usually no
  oven), microwave oven
レンズ lens
レンタカー car rental
レンタル rental
レントゲン Roentgen, X-ray

ローカル local
ローション lotion
ロースト roast
ローストチキン roast chicken
ロースハム roast ham
ロータリー rotary
ロードショー road show/premiere
  show (movies)
ローヒール low-heeled shoes
ロープ rope
ロープウエー ropeway, suspended
  cable car
ローマ Rome
ローラ Laura
ローラースケート roller skate(s)
ローリー Laurie
ロールスロイス Rolls-Royce
ローン loan
ロイヤル royal
ロケ on location (movie)
ロケット rocket; locket
ロサンゼルス Los Angeles
ロシア Russia
ロス Los Angeles; loss; Ross
ロダン Rodin
ロッカー locker
ロック rock (music); lock
ロビー lobby
ロブスター lobster
ロボット robot
ロマンス romance
ロマンチック romantic
ロレックス Rolex
ロング long (hair)
ロンジン Longines
ロンドン London

ワーグナー Wagner
ワープロ word processor
ワイキキ Waikiki
ワイシャツ dress shirt
ワイパー windshield wiper
ワイヤレスマイク wireless microphone
ワイン wine
ワクチン vaccine
ワゴン wagon
ワシントン Washington
ワックス wax
ワット watt
ワッペン (cloth) emblem
ワルツ waltz
ワンタン wonton
ワンピース one-piece dress
ワンマンカー bus with driver only, no
  ticket taker

# English–Katakana Glossary

AC-DC converter, adapter (electric power) アダプター
academy アカデミー
accelerator pedal アクセル
accent アクセント
accessory アクセサリー
accordion アコーディオン
acrobat アクロバット
acrylic アクリル
ad-lib アドリブ
adapter (electric power), AC-DC converter アダプター
adhesive cellophane tape セロテープ
advanced technology ハイテク
advice アドバイス
adviser アドバイザー
aerobics エアロビクス
Aesop イソップ
Africa アフリカ
Afro hairstyle アフロヘア
after-sales service アフターサービス
aftercare アフターケア
Aids エイズ
air conditioner エアコン
air conditioner, ice chest クーラー
airmail エアメール
a la carte アラカルト
Alaska アラスカ
album アルバム
alcohol アルコール
alibi アリバイ
alkali アルカリ
all-night オールナイト
allergy アレルギー
alphabet アルファベット
Alps アルプス
alterations (major) to clothing or a home リフォーム
aluminum アルミ、アルミニウム
amateur アマチュア
Amazon アマゾン

ambience, atmosphere ムード
amen アーメン
America アメリカ
ammonia アンモニア
amplifier, amp アンプ
Amsterdam アムステルダム
anchovy アンチョビ
Andersen アンデルセン
Andes アンデス
animated cartoon アニメ(ーション)
announcement (over a PA system) アナウンス
announcer アナウンサー
antenna アンテナ
apartment house アパート
appeal (let people know, request) アピール
apple pie アップルパイ
April Fools' Day エープリルフール
apron エプロン
Arab アラブ
Arabia アラビア
arcade アーケード
arch アーチ
Argentina アルゼンチン
Arizona アリゾナ
artist's studio アトリエ
Asia アジア
asparagus アスパラガス
asphalt アスファルト
aspirin アスピリン
assistant アシスタント
at one's own pace マイペース
Athens アテネ
athlete's shirt number ゼッケン
atmosphere, ambience ムード
attraction (program) アトラクション
auction オークション
audio オーディオ
audition (test) オーディション
aurora オーロラ

122

Australia　オーストラリア
auto race　オートレース
autograph, signature; signal　サイン
automatic locking door　オートロック
automation　オートメーション

baby boom　ベビーブーム
baby-sitter　ベビーシッター
Bach　バッハ
bacon　ベーコン
bacteria　バクテリア
badge　バッジ
balance　バランス
balcony　バルコニー
ballade　バラード
ballerina　バレリーナ
ballet　バレエ
ballpoint pen　ボールペン
banana　バナナ
band (brass)　ブラスバンド
band (music, watch)　バンド
bar (saloon)　バー、スナック
bar code　バーコード
bar manager (female); mamma, mom
　ママ
barbecue　バーベキュー
barbell　バーベル
bargain (sale)　バーゲン
barometer　バロメーター
baroque　バロック
barricade　バリケード
bartender　バーテン（ダー）
bass (vocal part); bath; bus　バス
bath towel　バスタオル
bath; bus; bass (vocal part)　バス
bathroom scale　ヘルスメーター
baton (conductor's)　タクト
Bavarian cream gelatin　ババロア
bazaar　バザー
beach towel　ビーチタオル
bead(s) (handicraft)　ビーズ
beaker　ビーカー
Beatles　ビートルズ
bed　ベッド
bed (double)　ダブル
bed (single)　シングル
bed (twin)　ツイン
bedroom community, suburbs　ベッド
　タウン

beef stroganoff　ビーフストロガノフ
beeper, pager　ポケットベル、ポケベル
beer　ビール
beer garden　ビアガーデン
beer mug　ジョッキ
Beethoven　ベートーベン
beige　ベージュ
Belgium　ベルギー
Bell　ベル
bell　ベル
belt　ベルト
belt (conveyor)　コンベヤーベルト
bench　ベンチ
benzine　ベンジン
Berlin　ベルリン
best seller　ベストセラー
best, vest　ベスト
beverage (thick fruit)　ネクター
bikini　ビキニ
bilingual　バイリンガル
Bill　ビル
billiards, pool　ビリヤード
biographical sketch (profile)　プロフィ
　ール
biscuit, (sweet) cracker　ビスケット
blacklist　ブラックリスト
blank (period of time)　ブランク
bleachers, desk/floor lamp　スタンド
blender; concrete mixer　ミキサー
blinds (Venetian)　ブラインド
blinker　ウインカー
block (cement)　ブロック
blouse　ブラウス
blow dry　ブロー
blues　ブルース
boat, rowboat　ボート
body guard　ボディーガード
body search / frisk　ボディーチェック
body-building　ボディービル
boiler　ボイラー
bolt, volt　ボルト
bonus　ボーナス
boom, fad　ブーム
boots　ブーツ
Boston　ボストン
Boston bag, overnight bag　ボストンバ
　ッグ
bottle (whiskey)　ボトル
bouquet　ブーケ

123

bourbon バーボン
boutique ブティック
bowling ボウリング
boxer ボクサー
boxing ボクシング
boy friend ボーイフレンド
Boy Scouts ボーイスカウト
boycott ボイコット
bracelet ブレスレット
Brahms ブラームス
brake (cars, bicycles, etc) ブレーキ
brake (hand/parking) サイドブレーキ
brand name (usually for expensive designer goods) ブランド
brandy ブランデー
brass band ブラスバンド
Brazil ブラジル
bread パン
broccoli ブロッコリー
brochure, pamphlet パンフレット
broker ブローカー
brooch ブローチ
brush ブラシ
bucket, pail バケツ
buffet バイキング
building (concrete), Bill ビル
buoy ブイ
bus with driver only, no ticket taker ワンマンカー
bus; bath; bass (vocal part) バス
business suit スーツ
businessman ビジネスマン
butter バター
buttered fish ムニエル
button ボタン
buzzer ブザー

cable car ケーブルカー
cable car (suspended) ロープウェー
cactus サボテン
caddie (golf) キャディー
caffeine カフェイン
café au lait カフェオレ
Cairo カイロ
cake ケーキ
cake (wedding) ウェディングケーキ
calcium カルシウム
calendar カレンダー
California カリフォルニア

calorie カロリー
cameo カメオ
camera カメラ
camera angle カメラアングル
cameraman, photographer カメラマン
camp キャンプ
campaign キャンペーン
campfire キャンプファイア
campus (usually college) キャンパス
canary カナリア
cancel, cancellation キャンセル
cane, walking stick ステッキ
canned tuna ツナ
canoe カヌー
capacity (exceeding), punk (rock), flat tire パンク
cape, mantle, cloak マント
capsule カプセル
captain キャプテン
car (privately owned) マイカー
car (sports) スポーツカー
car race オートレース
car rental レンタカー
car trunk トランク
caramel キャラメル
carbon (paper) カーボン
carbonated drink, soda ソーダ
card (credit etc., not playing cards) カード
cards (playing) トランプ
Carl, curl カール
carnation カーネーション
carpet カーペット
Cartier カルティエ
cartoon (animated) アニメ(ーション)
case ケース
cash card キャッシュカード
cash register レジ
cashmere カシミア
casserole グラタン
cassette tape カセットテープ
cast (of a play) キャスト
cast (plaster) ギプス
casual attire ラフ
catalog カタログ
catchword (slogan) キャッチフレーズ
Catholic カトリック
cauliflower カリフラワー
caviar キャビア

celery セロリ
Celine セリーヌ
cello チェロ
cellophane セロハン
cellophane tape (adhesive) セロテープ
cement セメント
cement block ブロック
cent セント
center line センターライン
centimeter センチ、センチメートル
cereal シリアル
Cessna (plane) セスナ
Chagall シャガール
chain チェーン
chalk チョーク
challenge チャレンジ
chameleon カメレオン
champagne シャンパン
champion チャンピオン
chance, opportunity チャンス
chandelier シャンデリア
Chanel シャネル
change one's image イメージチェンジ
channel (TV) チャンネル
chanson シャンソン
charity show チャリティーショー
charm point チャームポイント
charming チャーミング
charter (planes, etc.) チャーター
cheating on a written test カンニング
check in チェックイン
check-out チェックアウト
check point チェックポイント
cheese チーズ
cheese (process) プロセスチーズ
cheesecake チーズケーキ
chef シェフ
chef, cook コック
chess チェス
chestnut マロン
Chicago シカゴ
chicken (roast) ローストチキン
Chile チリ
chime チャイム
chocolate チョコレート
cholera コレラ
cholesterol コレステロール
Chopin ショパン
chord, cord, code コード

chorus コーラス
chowder チャウダー
Chris クリス
Christ キリスト
Christmas クリスマス
Christmas Eve クリスマスイブ
Christmas tree クリスマスツリー
cigarette タバコ
cinema シネマ
cinnamon シナモン
circle (club) サークル
circus サーカス
class クラス
classical music クラシック
classmate クラスメート
cleaning (dry) クリーニング
cleanser クレンザー
climax クライマックス
clip (paper/hair) クリップ
cloak, cape, mantle マント
cloakroom クローク
clover クローバー
clown ピエロ
club (group, playing cards) クラブ
coach コーチ
coaster コースター
cobra コブラ
Coca Cola コカコーラ
cocktail カクテル
cocoa, hot chocolate ココア
Cocteau コクトー
code, chord, cord コード
coffee コーヒー
coffee (iced) アイスコーヒー
coffee (instant) インスタントコーヒー
coffee cream, milk ミルク
coffee-flavored gelatin コーヒーゼリー
coin-operated locker コインロッカー
cola コーラ
collect call コレクトコール
college students' party コンパ
cologne オーデコロン
Cologne ケルン
color (TV, photo) カラー
Columbus コロンブス
comedian コメディアン
comment コメント
commercial コマーシャル
communication コミュニケーション

community コミュニティー
compact コンパクト
compasses コンパス
competitive bid, tournament (golf) コンペ
complaint (for damages, etc.) クレーム
computer コンピュータ(ー)
concert コンサート
concert hall コンサートホール
concrete (cement) コンクリート
concrete building, Bill ビル
concrete mixer; blender ミキサー
condition (one's body) コンディション
condominium マンション
condom コンドーム
conductor's baton タクト
cone (ice cream); corn コーン
consommè コンソメ
consultant コンサルタント
consumer tester, monitor (TV) モニター
contact lens コンタクトレンズ
contest コンテスト
control コントロール
convenience store コンビニ(エンス ストア)
converter (AC-DC), adapter (electric power) アダプター
convertible (open) オープンカー
conveyor (belt) コンベヤーベルト
cook (professional), chef コック
cooked rice (on a plate) ライス
cookie クッキー
copy (usually photocopy) コピー
copywriter コピーライター
cord, chord, code コード
cordless コードレス
cork コルク
corn potage, cream of corn soup コーンポタージュ
corn soup (cream of) コーンポタージュ
corn; cone (ice cream) コーン
cornflakes コーンフレーク
cornstarch コーンスターチ
cosmetics (make-up) メイク
counseling カウンセリング
counselor カウンセラー
counter カウンター
counter or section (special) コーナー
coup d'état クーデター

couple (dating) アベック
couple (male and female) カップル
coupon クーポン
cover, covering カバー
cracker (soda) クラッカー
cracker (sweet), biscuit ビスケット
crane (machine) クレーン
crawl (swimming stroke) クロール
crayon クレヨン
cream クリーム
cream (sour) サワークリーム
cream of corn soup, corn potage コーンポタージュ
cream puff シュークリーム
credit (payment) クレジット
credit card クレジットカード
crepe クレープ
crib ベビーベッド
croissant クロワッサン
croquette コロッケ
cruiser (cabin) クルーザー
cuff, cuff link カフス
culottes キュロット
culture shock カルチャーショック
cup (coffee, tea; trophy) カップ
Curie キュリー
curl; Carl カール
curler カーラー
curry on rice カレーライス
cursor カーソル
curtain カーテン
curve カーブ
cushion クッション
custard pudding プリン
custom made オーダーメード
cut (hair; movie) カット
cycling サイクリング
Cézanne セザンヌ

da Vinci ダ・ビンチ
dam ダム
dance ダンス
dancer ダンサー
Darwin ダーウィン
data データ
date (boy-girl) デート
dating couple アベック、カップル
Debussy ドビュッシー
debut デビュー

126

delicate デリケート
deluxe デラックス
demonstration (protest) デモ
denim デニム
department store デパート
design デザイン
designer デザイナー
desk/floor lamp, bleachers スタンド
dessert デザート
dial ダイヤル
diamond ダイヤ（モンド）
diesel ディーゼル
diet (weight control) ダイエット
digital デジタル
dilemma ジレンマ
dinette ダイニングキッチン
dining room ダイニング
Dior ディオール
director ディレクター
disco ディスコ
discount price, free of charge, service
　サービス
Disneyland ディズニーランド
diving ダイビング
documentary (film) ドキュメンタリー
dollar ドル
dome ドーム
domino ドミノ
door ドア
Dostoyevski ドストエフスキー
double(whiskey; bed) ダブル
doubles (tennis) ダブルス
doughnut ドーナツ
Dracula, vampire ドラキュラ
drama (TV, radio) ドラマ
drawing (sketch) デッサン
dress ドレス
dress (expensive ready-made) プレタポ
　ルテ
dress (wedding) ウェディングドレス
dress shirt ワイシャツ
dressing (salad) ドレッシング
driver on paper only, licensed non-
　driver ペーパードライバー
driving for pleasure ドライブ
drum ドラム
dry (blow) ブロー
dry cleaning クリーニング
dry ice ドライアイス

dubbing (film, tape) ダビング
duet デュエット
dump truck ダンプカー
Dunhill ダンヒル
duo, well-matched pair (people) コンビ
dynamite ダイナマイト

earphone イヤホーン
earring イヤリング
earrings (pierced) ピアス
Easter イースター
economy class (on planes) エコノミー
　クラス
éclair エクレア
Edison エジソン
egoist, egotist エゴイスト
Egypt エジプト
Einstein アインシュタイン
electric plug プラグ
electric switch スイッチ
elegant エレガント
elementary school student's hard
　leather knapsack ランドセル
elevator エレベーター
elite (person) エリート
emblem (cloth) ワッペン
enamel エナメル
encore アンコール
energy エネルギー
engagement ring エンゲージリング
engine エンジン
engine (stalled) エンスト
engineer エンジニア
ensemble アンサンブル
episode エピソード
error (computer, baseball) エラー
escalator エスカレーター
Eskimo エスキモー
etiquette エチケット
Eurasia ユーラシア
Europe ヨーロッパ
exaggeration (overdone), overcoat オ
　ーバー
exchange rate レート
experience (working, career) キャリア
extra (in a movie) エキストラ
eye shadow アイシャドー
eyeliner アイライン

fad, boom ブーム
fair play フェアプレー
false rumor デマ
family restaurant/diner ファミリーレストラン
fan ファン
fan heater ファンヒーター
fanatic (e.g., car freak) マニア
fanfare ファンファーレ
fantasy ファンタジー
fashion ファッション
fashion stylist スタイリスト
fast-food ファーストフード
fax ファ(ッ)クス
felt (cloth) フェルト
felt pen サインペン
feminist, gallant man フェミニスト
fencing (sport) フェンシング
ferry フェリー
fiancé, fiancée フィアンセ
fiber glass ファイバーグラス
fiberscope ファイバースコープ
fiction フィクション
fighting spirit, fervor ファイト
file (papers) ファイル
filet ヒレ
filet steak, tenderloin steak ヒレステーキ
film (roll) フィルム
film production プロダクション
filter フィルター
finale (stage show) フィナーレ
finder (view) ファインダー
first class (plane and boat seats) ファーストクラス
fish (buttered) ムニエル
fitness フィットネス
flamenco フラメンコ
flamingo フラミンゴ
flannel ネル
flared skirt フレアスカート
flash (photography) フラッシュ
flat tire, over-full capacity, punk (rock) パンク
flight (airplane) フライト
floor (wooden) フローリング
floor/desk lamp, bleachers スタンド
floppy (disk) フロッピー
flute フルート
fly (baseball) フライ

focus (camera) ピント
foil (aluminum) ホイル
folk dance フォークダンス
folk music, fork フォーク
font フォント
folk song フォークソング
foot/feet (measurement) フィート
football フットボール
fork; folk music フォーク
formal フォーマル
frame (bowling, eyeglass) フレーム
France フランス
Frankfurt フランクフルト
free of charge, service, discount price サービス
free pass フリーパス
freeway off/on ramp ランプ
French bread フランスパン
French fries フライドポテト
fried chicken フライドチキン
frill フリル
frisbee フリズビー
frisk, body search ボディーチェック
front desk (in hotel) フロント
fruit フルーツ
fruit beverage (thick) ネクター
frying pan フライパン
full time フルタイム
full-course フルコース
fund raising campaign/collection カンパ
fuse ヒューズ

gag (joke) ギャグ
Galileo ガリレオ
gallant man, feminist フェミニスト
gallery (art), spectators ギャラリー
gamble, gambling ギャンブル
game (other than sports) ゲーム
game of "catch" キャッチボール
gangster ギャング
gas ガス
gas station, service station ガソリンスタンド
gasoline ガソリン
gate (airport, horse race starting) ゲート
gauze ガーゼ
gelatin (Bavarian cream) ババロア
gelatin (coffee-flavored) コーヒーゼリー
gelatin (substance) ゼラチン

gelatin dessert ゼリー
genre ジャンル
George ジョージ
German mark マルク
Germany ドイツ
gift ギフト
gift (present) プレゼント
gin ジン
girl friend ガールフレンド
Girl Scout (the Girl Scouts) ガールスカ
ウト
Givenchy ジバンシィ
glass (drinking/water) コップ
glass (the material) ガラス
glass (whisky/wine) グラス
glider (plane) グライダー
glove (boxing, baseball) グローブ
Goethe ゲーテ
goggles ゴーグル
Golden Week holidays (Apr. 29–May
5) ゴールデンウィーク
golf ゴルフ
golf caddie キャディー
gorilla ゴリラ
gossip ゴシップ
gourmet グルメ
grapefruit グレープフルーツ
graph グラフ
Greece ギリシャ
green pepper ピーマン
greenhouse (plastic) ビニールハウス
grill グリル
Grimm グリム
grotesque グロテスク
grounds グラ(ウ)ンド
group グループ
guard; railroad trestle ガード
Gucci グッチ
guerrilla ゲリラ
guest ゲスト
guide ガイド
guinea pig モルモット
guitar ギター
gum (chewing) ガム
guppy グッピー

hair (long) ロング
hair (short) ショート
hair cream ヘアクリーム

hair dryer ドライヤー
hair tonic ヘアトニック
hairpiece ヘアピース
hairpin ヘアピン
hairstyle ヘアスタイル
half time ハーフタイム
hallelujah ハレルヤ
Halloween ハロウィーン
ham ハム
ham (roast) ロースハム
ham sandwich ハムサンド
hamburger (with bun) ハンバーガー
hamburger cutlet メンチカツ
hamburger steak ハンバーグ
hammer ハンマー
hammock ハンモック
hand/parking brake サイドブレーキ
handbag, purse (ハンド)バッグ
handbook (manual) マニュアル
handkerchief ハンカチ
handlebars; steering wheel ハンドル
handsome (man) ハンサム
hanger ハンガー
hard disk ハードディスク
harmonica ハーモニカ
harp ハープ
Hawaii ハワイ
Haydn ハイドン
headphone ヘッドホン
hearts (playing cards) ハート
heater ストーブ、ヒーター
heavy smoker ヘビースモーカー
hectare ヘクタール
heel (shoe) ヒール
Heine ハイネ
Helen Keller ヘレン ケラー
helicopter ヘリコプター
helmet ヘルメット
Hemingway ヘミングウェー
Henry ヘンリー
Hermes エルメス
hernia ヘルニア
Hertz ヘルツ
Hesse ヘッセ
hi-fi ハイファイ
high-heeled shoes ハイヒール
highlight ハイライト
hijacking ハイジャック
hiker ハイカー

hiking ハイキング
Himalaya ヒマラヤ
hint ヒント
hip(s), hipline ヒップ
hired taxi ハイヤー
hit chart (music) ヒットチャート
hitchhike ヒッチハイク
Holland オランダ
home (privately owned) マイホーム
home plate ホーム
home run ホームラン
homeroom ホームルーム
homesickness ホームシック
honeymoon ハネムーン
Honolulu ホノルル
hood (car) ボンネット
hook (garment) ホック
hormone ホルモン
horn (car) クラクション
hors d'oeuvre オードブル
hose (water) ホース
host ホスト
hostel (youth) ユースホステル
hostess (bar) ホステス
hot chocolate, cocoa ココア
hot coffee ホットコーヒー
hot tea with lemon レモンティー
hot tea with milk/cream ミルクティー
hotcake, pancake ホットケーキ
hotel ホテル
hotel (inexpensive) mainly used on
  business trips ビジネスホテル
hotel (inexpensive) with capsule-
  shaped sleeping compartments カプ
  セルホテル
house paint ペンキ
humor ユーモア
humorous ユーモラス
hunger strike ハンスト、ハンガースト
  ライキ
hurdle ハードル
hurricane ハリケーン
hyphen ハイフン
hysteria ヒステリー

Ibsen イプセン
ice (dry) ドライアイス
ice chest, air conditioner クーラー
ice cream アイスクリーム

ice cream (soft) ソフトクリーム
ice cream parfait アイスクリームパフェ
ice cream sundae アイスクリームサン
  デー
ice hockey アイスホッケー
ice skating スケート、アイススケート
iced coffee アイスコーヒー
iced tea アイスティー
Idaho アイダホ
idea アイデア
ignition key エンジンキー
Illinois イリノイ
illumination イルミネーション
illustration イラスト
illustrator イラストレーター
image イメージ
image (change of one's) イメージチェ
  ンジ
imbalance, unbalanced アンバランス
imitation イミテーション
inch インチ
Indian (American) インディアン
Indonesia インドネシア
inferiority complex コンプレックス
inflation インフレ
influenza インフルエンザ
informal インフォーマル
information (desk) インフォメーション
initials (personal) イニシャル
ink インク
instant インスタント
instant coffee インスタントコーヒー
intellectual インテリ
inter high school athletic competition
  インターハイ
intercom, interphone インタホン
interior decorations インテリア
intern インターン
international インターナショナル
interphone, intercom インタホン
interview インタビュー
intonation イントネーション
introduction (musical) イントロ
ion イオン
Iowa アイオワ
Iran イラン
Iraq イラク
Ireland アイルランド
iron (for pressing clothes) アイロン

130

Israel イスラエル
Italy イタリア

jacket ジャケット
jacket (casual) ジャンパー
jam (fruit) ジャム
jazz ジャズ
jeans ジーンズ、ジーパン
jeep ジープ
Jerusalem エルサレム
Jewish, Judea ユダヤ
jinx, superstition ジンクス
jogging ジョギング
journalist ジャーナリスト
Judea, Jewish ユダヤ
juice ジュース
jukebox ジュークボックス
jumper (dress) ジャンパースカート
jungle ジャングル

kangaroo カンガルー
Kenya ケニア
ketchup ケチャップ
key (ignition) エンジンキー
key chain キーホルダー
keyboard キーボード
kilogram キログラム
kilometer キロ、キロメートル
kiss キス
kitchen range (usually no oven),
  microwave oven レンジ
kiwi キウイ
kleenex ティッシュ(ペーパー)
knapsack (elementary school student's
  hard leather) ランドセル
knife ナイフ
knife (surgical) メス
knitwear ニット
knock (on a door) ノック
knockout ノックアウト
koala コアラ

label ラベル
labor strike スト、ストライキ
lace; race レース
ladies first レディーファースト
lamb (meat), rum ラム
lamination ラミネート
lamp (desk/floor); bleachers スタンド

lamp (oil/kerosene) ランプ
Laos ラオス
Larry; (car) rally ラリー
Las Vegas ラスベガス
laser レーザー
laser disc レーザーディスク
last order (food/drinks) オーダーストッ
  プ、ラストオーダー
laundromat, launderette コインランド
  リー
Laura ローラ
Laurie ローリー
layout (book etc.) レイアウト
lead, reed (instrument) リード
leader リーダー
leadership リーダーシップ
league (baseball) リーグ
leisure time amusement, recreation レ
  ジャー
lemon レモン
lemon soda レモンスカッシュ
lens レンズ
lens (contact) コンタクトレンズ
lens (zoom) ズームレンズ
leotard(s) レオタード
lettuce レタス
level レベル
lever, liver レバー
lifework ライフワーク
lift (ski) リフト
light(s) (stage, car) ライト
lighter (cigarette) ライター
lightweight class (boxing) ライト
Lima リマ
lime ライム
limousine リムジン
lion ライオン
liqueur リキュール
liquor glass (whiskey, wine) グラス
lira リラ
list リスト
Liszt リスト
live music ライブ
liver, lever レバー
living room リビング
loan ローン
lobby ロビー
lobster ロブスター
local ローカル

location (movie) ロケ
lock; rock (music) ロック
locker ロッカー
locker (coin-operated) コインロッカー
locket; rocket ロケット
locking door (automatic) オートロック
London ロンドン
long (hair) ロング
Longines ロンジン
Los Angeles ロス、ロサンゼルス
loss; Ross; Los Angeles ロス
lotion ローション
lounge ラウンジ
love letter ラブレター
low-heeled shoes ローヒール
lunch ランチ

Macao マカオ
macaroni マカロニ
magic marker マジックペン
mail box (on street corner); post
  (position) ポスト
make-up (cosmetics) メイク
Malaysia マレーシア
mamma, mom; female bar manager ママ
mammoth マンモス
manager (store) マネージャー
manhole マンホール
Manila マニラ
mannequin マネキン
manners マナー
mantle, cloak, cape マント
manual (handbook) マニュアル
manufacturer メーカー
maple (or sugar) syrup シロップ
marathon マラソン
march マーチ
margarine マーガリン
Mark (name); a mark マーク
marketing マーケティング
marmalade ママレード
marriage proposal プロポーズ
Marx マルクス
Mary メアリー、メリー
mascara マスカラ
mascot マスコット
mask (gauze, respirator) マスク
masking tape ガムテープ
mass media マスコミ

massage マッサージ
mast マスト
match (for fire) マッチ
mattress マットレス
Maupassant モーパッサン
May Day メーデー
mayonnaise マヨネーズ
McDonald's マクドナルド
meat sauce (for spaghetti) ミートソース
mechanical pencil シャープペン(シル)
medal メダル
medley メドレー
megaphone メガホン
melody メロディー
melon メロン
member メンバー
memo メモ
memory (computer) メモリー
Mendelssohn メンデルスゾーン
menu メニュー
Mercedes-Benz ベンツ
merit メリット
Merry Christmas メリークリスマス
message メッセージ
metal メタル
meter メートル
meter (gauge) メーター
metronome メトロノーム
Mexico メキシコ
Miami マイアミ
Michelangelo ミケランジェロ
Michigan ミシガン
microcomputer マイコン
microphone (wireless) ワイヤレスマイク
microphone; Mike マイク
microwave oven, kitchen range
  (usually no oven) レンジ
Mike; microphone マイク
Milano ミラノ
mile マイル
milk, coffee cream ミルク
Millet ミレー
millimeter ミリメートル
mineral ミネラル
mineral water ミネラルウォーター
miniature ミニチュア
miniskirt ミニスカート
mink ミンク
Minnesota ミネソタ

132

mint ミント
minus マイナス
Miro ミロ
mirror (rear-view) バックミラー
misprint ミスプリント
Miss Universe ミスユニバース
Miss; mistake ミス
missile ミサイル
mission school ミッションスクール
mistake; Miss ミス
mixed (finger) sandwiches ミックスサンド
mocha (coffee) モカ
model モデル
model (plastic) プラモデル
mohair モヘア
mom ママ
Monaco モナコ
Monet モネ
monitor (TV), consumer tester モニター
monochrome モノクロ
monorail モノレール
Montreal モントリオール
Moscow モスクワ
mothball, naphthalene ナフタリン
motor モーター
motorbike, motorcycle バイク、オートバイ
motto モットー
mousse (dessert, hair cream) ムース
movie location ロケ
movie production プロダクション
movie screen スクリーン
movie star's or singer's still picture ブロマイド
movie subtitle , supermarket スーパー
Mozart モーツァルト
Mrs. ミセス
muffler; winter scarf マフラー
mug (beer) ジョッキ
mummy ミイラ
mushroom マッシュルーム
music (live ) ライブ
music (pop) ポップス
music (popular) ポピュラー
music (rock); lock ロック
music box オルゴール
music solo ソロ
musical (play) ミュージカル

musical introduction イントロ
mustard マスタード
mutton マトン
muumuu ムームー
mystery ミステリー

nail polish マニキュア
naive ナイーブ
Nancy ナンシー
naphthalene, mothball ナフタリン
napkin ナプキン
Napoleon ナポレオン
narration ナレーション
narrator ナレーター
necklace ネックレス
necktie ネクタイ
negative (film) ネガ
neon ネオン
nervous breakdown, neurosis ノイローゼ
network ネットワーク
neurosis, nervous breakdown ノイローゼ
New York ニューヨーク
newscaster ニュースキャスター
Newton ニュートン
Niagara ナイアガラ
Nice ニース
nickname ニックネーム
nicotine ニコチン
night game ナイター
Nile ナイル
Nina Ricci ニナ　リッチ
Nixon ニクソン
no comment ノーコメント
Nobel ノーベル
nominate ノミネート
nonsense ナンセンス
noodles in hot soup (ramen) ラーメン
norm, production quota (assigned) ノルマ
normal ノーマル
Norway ノルウェー
notebook ノート
nuance ニュアンス
nude ヌード
number (athlete's shirt) ゼッケン
nut ナッツ
nylon ナイロン
nylon stockings ストッキング

oasis オアシス
oatmeal オートミール
occult オカルト
occurrence (unexpected) ハプニング
octave オクターブ
off-season シーズン・オフ
oil オイル
oil change オイルチェンジ
Okhotsk オホーツク
Oklahoma オクラホマ
okra オクラ
olive オリーブ
Olympics オリンピック
Omega オメガ
omelet オムレツ
on the rocks オンザロック
one size fits all フリーサイズ
one-on-one マンツーマン
one-piece dress ワンピース
opal オパール
open convertible (car) オープンカー
opera オペラ
opera glasses オペラグラス
operator (telephone) オペレーター
opportunity, chance チャンス
orange (color, fruit) オレンジ
orchestra オーケストラ
organ (reed) オルガン
original オリジナル
Othello オセロ
ounce オンス
oven オーブン
overcoat オーバー
overdone (exaggeration) オーバー
overnight bag, Boston bag ボストンバッグ
owner オーナー

pace (at one's own) マイペース
paddle (ping-pong) ラケット
page (book) ページ
pager, beeper ポケットベル、ポケベル
pail, bucket バケツ
paint (house) ペンキ
pair (two people) ペア
pair (two well-matched people), a duo, コンビ
pajamas パジャマ
pamphlet, brochure パンフレット

pancake, hotcake ホットケーキ
panda パンダ
panel パネル
panic パニック
panorama パノラマ
pantomime パントマイム
pants, trousers ズボン
panty hose パンスト
papa パパ
paper towel ペーパータオル
parachute パラシュート
parade パレード
parfait (ice cream) パフェ、アイスクリームパフェ
Paris パリ
parody パロディー
parsley パセリ
part-time パート、パートタイム
partner パートナー
party パーティー
party (college students) コンパ
pass パス
passport パスポート
pasta パスタ
patient's hospital chart カルテ
patrol パトロール
patrol car (police) パトカー
pause, pose ポーズ
Pavlov パブロフ
peak ピーク
peanut ピーナッツ
peanut butter ピーナッツバター
pedal ペダル
pelican ペリカン
pen name ペンネーム
pen pal ペンパル
pendant ペンダント
penguin ペンギン
penicillin ペニシリン
peppermint ペパーミント
percent パーセント
permanent wave, perm パーマ
personal computer パソコン
personality (TV) タレント
pet (animal) ペット
pet food ペットフード
philharmony フィルハーモニー
Philippines フィリピン
photographer, cameraman カメラマン

Piaget ピアジェ
pianist ピアニスト
piano ピアノ
Picasso ピカソ
picnic ピクニック
pie パイ
pierced earrings ピアス
pilaf ピラフ
pilot (aircraft) パイロット
pinchers, pliers ペンチ
pineapple パイナップル
ping-pong ピンポン
pipe パイプ
pistol ピストル
pizza ピザ
pizza sauce and cheese on toast ピザトースト
placard プラカード
plan プラン
planetarium プラネタリウム
plankton プランクトン
plaster cast ギプス
plastic プラスチック
plastic greenhouse ビニールハウス
plastic model (toy) プラモデル
plastic (bag), vinyl ビニール
platform (train) ホーム
platinum プラチナ
playing cards トランプ
pleats プリーツ
pliers, pinchers ペンチ
plug (electric) プラグ
plus プラス
plus (something plus a little more) プラスアルファ
plywood, veneer ベニヤ
pocket ポケット
poker ポーカー
poker face ポーカーフェース
Polaroid ポラロイド
polo shirt ポロシャツ
polyester ポリエステル
pool (swimming) プール
pool, billiards ビリヤード
pop music ポップス
popcorn ポップコーン
popular music ポピュラー
popular teenage singer アイドル
portable ポータブル

porter ポーター
pose, pause ポーズ
post (position); mail box (on street corner etc.) ポスト
poster ポスター
potage (corn) コーンポタージュ
potage (soup) ポタージュ
potato chip(s) ポテトチップ
prefabricated structure プレハブ
premiere show (movies)/road show ロードショー
premium プレミア(ム)
present (gift) プレゼント
pressure (psychological) プレッシャー
pride プライド
prime time ゴールデンアワー
printer (computer) プリンタ（ー）
prism プリズム
privacy プライバシー
private プライベート
privately owned car マイカー
privately owned home マイホーム
process cheese プロセスチーズ
producer プロデューサー
production (film) プロダクション
production quota (assigned), norm ノルマ
professional wrestling プロレス
professional; production (film) プロ
profile (biographical sketch) プロフィール
program プログラム
program of entertainments イベント
programmer (computer) プログラマー
project プロジェクト
propane gas プロパンガス
propeller プロペラ
proposal (marriage) プロポーズ
protest (demonstration) デモ
psychological stress ストレス
pub パブ
pudding (custard) プリン
pulp (wood) パルプ
pump ポンプ
pumps (shoes) パンプス
punk (rock); flat tire; over-full capacity パンク
purse, handbag （ハンド）バッグ
push button phone プッシュホン

135

puzzle パズル
pyramid ピラミッド

questionnaire アンケート
quiz クイズ

race; lace レース
racer レーサー
racket (tennis) ラケット
radar レーダー
radio ラジオ
radio cassette player ラジカセ
radio control (toy/models) ラジコン
rail レール
railroad trestle; guard ガード
raincoat レインコート
raisin レーズン
rally (car); Larry ラリー
ramen (Chinese noodles in hot soup) ラーメン
ramp (freeway on/off) ランプ
rate (of exchange) レート
rayon レーヨン
ready-made (expensive) dress プレタポルテ
rear-view mirror バックミラー
rebate リベート
receipt レシート
receiver (electric wave) レシーバー
recital リサイタル
reclining seat リクライニングシート
record (music) レコード
recreation, leisure time amusement レジャー
recruit リクルート
recycle リサイクル
reed (instrument); lead リード
regular (member) レギュラー
rehabilitation リハビリ
rehearsal リハーサル
relax リラックス
relay (race) リレー
remote control リモコン
Renoir ルノワール
rental レンタル
rent-a-car レンタカー
repertory レパートリー
report レポート/リポート
reputable brand name (usually for

expensive designer goods) ブランド
request (usually songs) リクエスト
reserved seating on trains for elderly
and handicapped (silver seat) シルバーシート
resort リゾート
restaurant レストラン
restroom, toilet トイレ
revival リバイバル
revue レビュー
rheumatism リューマチ
rhythm リズム
ribbon リボン
rice (served on a plate) ライス
rice casserole ドリア
rice omelet オムライス
rifle ライフル
ring (engagement) エンゲージリング
rink リンク
rinse (for hair) リンス
risk リスク
rival ライバル
road show/premiere show (movies) ロードショー
roast ロースト
roast chicken ローストチキン
roast ham ロースハム
robot ロボット
rock (music); lock ロック
rocket; locket ロケット
rocks (on the) オンザロック
Rodin ロダン
roe (salted salmon) イクラ
Roentgen (X-ray) レントゲン
Rolex ロレックス
roller coaster ジェットコースター
roller skate(s) ローラースケート
Rolls-Royce ロールスロイス
romance ロマンス
Romania ルーマニア
romantic ロマンチック
Rome ローマ
roommate ルームメート
rope ロープ
ropeway ロープウエー
Ross; Los Angeles; loss ロス
rotary ロータリー
rouge ルージュ
roulette ルーレット

Rousseau ルソー
rowboat, boat ボート
royal ロイヤル
rubber ゴム
rubber stamp スタンプ
ruby ルビー
rugby ラグビー
rule ルール
rum; lamb (meat) ラム
runner ランナー
rush hour ラッシュアワー
Russia ロシア

safari park サファリパーク
safe セーフ
sailboat, yacht ヨット
Saint Laurent サンローラン
salad サラダ
salad dressing ドレッシング
salami サラミ
sale (bargain) セール、バーゲン
salmon roe (salted) イクラ
salon サロン
salted salmon roe イクラ
samba サンバ
Samoa サモア
sample (product) サンプル
San Francisco サンフランシスコ
sandal(s) サンダル
sandwich サンドイッチ
sandwiches (mixed finger) ミックスサンド
Santa Claus サンタクロース
sapphire サファイア
satin サテン
sauce (usually Worcestershire) ソース
sauna サウナ
sausage ソーセージ
sauté ソテー
scale (relative size and degree) スケール
scandal スキャンダル
scarf スカーフ
scarf (winter), muffler マフラー
scenario シナリオ
scene シーン
schedule スケジュール
school knapsack (elementary school student's hard leather) ランドセル

Schubert シューベルト
Schumann シューマン
Schweitzer シュバイツァー
scoop (news) スクープ
scooter スクーター
score スコア
Scotch スコッチ
Scotch tape (adhesive cellophane tape) セロテープ
screen (movie) スクリーン
searchlight サーチライト
season シーズン
seat belt シートベルト
Seattle シアトル
section or counter (special) コーナー
security guard, watchman ガードマン
seesaw シーソー
Seine セーヌ
self-service セルフサービス
seminar セミナー
sensor センサー
sentimental センチメンタル
Seoul; soul music ソウル
series シリーズ
serve (ball) サーブ
service station, gas station ガソリンスタンド
service, discount price, free of charge サービス
sewing machine ミシン
sexual harassment セクハラ
Shakespeare シェークスピア
shampoo シャンプー
sheet(s) (bed) シーツ
sherbet シャーベット
sherry シェリー
shift (keyboard) シフト
shirt (dress) ワイシャツ
shirt (polo) ポロシャツ
shirt, undershirt シャツ
shopping ショッピング
short (hair) ショート
shortcake (usually strawberry) ショートケーキ
shovel シャベル、スコップ
shower シャワー
showroom ショールーム
shutter (camera, door) シャッター
Siberia シベリア

side job アルバイト,バイト
signal; signature, autograph サイン
signature; autograph; signal サイン
silk シルク
silo サイロ
silver seat (seats nominally reserved on trains for the elderly or disabled) シルバーシート
single (whiskey; bed) シングル
singles (tennis) シングルス
siren サイレン
sirloin steak サーロインステーキ
size サイズ
size (one size fits all) フリーサイズ
skating (ice) スケート
sketch (drawing) デッサン
ski lift スキーリフト
ski poles ストック
ski slope ゲレンデ
ski(s), skiing スキー
skirt スカート
skiwear スキーウェア
skunk スカンク
slender (i.e., stylish and smart) スマート
slide (photography) スライド
slippers (indoor) スリッパ
slogan (catchword) スローガン
slow motion スローモーション
slum スラム
smart (i.e., stylish, slender) スマート
smog スモッグ
smoker (heavy) ヘビースモーカー
sneaker スニーカー
snorkel スノーケル
snow tire スノータイヤ
soccer サッカー
sock(s) ソックス
soda, carbonated drink ソーダ
sofa ソファー
soft ice cream ソフトクリーム
software ソフト
solo (music) ソロ
something plus a little more プラスアルファ
Sony ソニー
soprano ソプラノ
soul music; Seoul ソウル
soup スープ
soup (cream of corn; corn potage) コー

ンポタージュ
sour cream サワークリーム
Soviet Union ソビエト
space スペース
spade (playing cards) スペード
spaghetti スパゲティ
Spain スペイン
speaker (audio) スピーカー
special counter or section コーナー
speech スピーチ
speed スピード
sponge スポンジ
sponsor スポンサー
spoon スプーン
sport スポーツ
sports car スポーツカー
sportsman スポーツマン
spotlight スポットライト
spray スプレー
spy スパイ
stadium スタジアム
stage ステージ
stained glass ステンドグラス
stainless steel ステンレス
stalled engine エンスト
stamina スタミナ
stamp (rubber) スタンプ
stapler ホッチキス
star (performer) スター
start スタート
starting line スタートライン
steak ステーキ
steak (hamburger) ハンバーグ
steak (sirloin) サーロインステーキ
steak (tenderloin, filet) ヒレステーキ
steam iron スチームアイロン
steering wheel; handlebars ハンドル
stereo ステレオ
stew シチュー
stewardess スチュワーデス
stick (walking), cane ステッキ
sticker シール
still picture (of movie star or singer) ブロマイド
stopwatch ストップウォッチ
storage room トランクルーム
straight (game score, whiskey) ストレート
Strauss シュトラウス

straw (for drinking) ストロー
stress (psychological) ストレス
strike (baseball, bowling) ストライク
strike (hunger) ハンスト, ハンガーストライキ
strike (labor) スト, ストライキ
stroganoff (beef) ビーフストロガノフ
stroller ベビーカー
studio (not apartment) スタジオ
stunt man スタントマン
style (fashion); one's figure スタイル
stylish (i.e., slender and smart) スマート
subtitle (movie); supermarket スーパー
suburbs, bedroom community ベッドタウン
Sue スー
sugar (or maple) syrup シロップ
suit (business) スーツ
suitcase スーツケース
summer school サマースクール
sundae (ice cream) アイスクリームサンデー
sunglasses サングラス
superman スーパーマン
supermarket; movie subtitle スーパー
surfboard サーフボード
surfer サーファー
surfing サーフィング
surgical knife メス
suspended cable car ロープウェー
sweat pants/suit ジャージー
sweat shirt トレーナー
sweater セーター
Sweden スウェーデン
swimming pool プール
swing ブランコ
switch (electric) スイッチ
Switzerland スイス
Sydney シドニー
symbol シンボル
symphony シンフォニー
symposium シンポジウム
synchronized swimming シンクロ(ナイズドスイミング)
synthesizer シンセサイザー
syrup (maple; sugar) シロップ
system システム

T-shirt ティーシャツ

tab (keyboard) タブ
Tabasco タバスコ
table (furniture) テーブル
taboo タブー
Tahiti タヒチ
tango タンゴ
tank (gas etc.) タンク
tanker タンカー
tape テープ
tape recorder テープレコーダー
Tarzan ターザン
taxi タクシー
taxi (hired) ハイヤー
tea (hot, with lemon) レモンティー
tea (hot, with milk/cream) ミルクティー
tea (iced) アイスティー
team チーム
teamwork チームワーク
technique テクニック
technology テクノロジー
teenage idol アイドル
telepathy テレパシー
television テレビ
tempo テンポ
tenderloin steak, filet steak ヒレステーキ
Tennessee テネシー
tennis テニス
tennis court テニスコート
tennis racket ラケット
tent テント
tequila テキーラ
terminal (airport, bus) ターミナル
terrace テラス
terrorism テロ
test テスト
Texas テキサス
textbook テキスト
Thailand タイ
theater ticket agency プレイガイド
theme テーマ
thermos bottle ポット
Thomas トーマス
thrill スリル
thyme; time タイム
ticket agency (for theater) プレイガイド
tiepin, tie tack ネクタイピン
Tiffany ティファニー
tile タイル
time; thyme タイム

timeout タイムアウト
timer タイマー
timetable (train or plane) ダイヤ
timing タイミング
tinplate ブリキ
tip (gratuity) チップ
tire タイヤ
tissue paper ティッシュ(ペーパー)
toast (bread) トースト
toast (pizza sauce and cheese on) ピザ
　トースト
toaster トースター
toaster oven オーブントースター
toilet paper トイレットペーパー
toilet, restroom トイレ
toll free call フリーダイヤル
Tolstoy トルストイ
Tom トム
tomato トマト
tomato sauce with vegetables
　(spaghetti) ナポリタン
ton トン
topic トピック
tough, healthy, sturdy (person) タフ
tour ツアー
tournament トーナメント
tournament (golf), competitive bid コ
　ンペ
towel タオル
towel (beach) ビーチタオル
towel (paper) ペーパータオル
tower タワー
track, truck トラック
tractor トラクター
trademark トレードマーク
trailer トレーラー
train platform ホーム
training トレーニング
trampoline トランポリン
treatment (for hair) トリートメント
trio トリオ
trophy トロフィー
tropical トロピカル
trousers, pants ズボン
truck (dump) ダンプカー
truck; track トラック
trumpet トランペット
trunk (car) トランク
Tschaikovsky チャイコフスキー

tube チューブ
tuna (canned) ツナ
tunnel トンネル
turtleneck タートルネック
tuxedo タキシード
TV channel チャンネル
TV personality タレント
tweezers ピンセット
twin (bed) ツイン
type タイプ
typewriter タイプライター

U-turn ユーターン
ukulele ウクレレ
unbalanced, imbalance アンバランス
underpants パンツ
undershirt, shirt シャツ
UNESCO ユネスコ
unexpected occurrence ハプニング
UNICEF ユニセフ
uniform (sports) ユニホーム
unique ユニーク
United Kingdom イギリス
Utah ユタ

vaccine ワクチン
Valentine's Day バレンタインデー
vampire, Dracula ドラキュラ
Van Gogh ゴッホ
varnish ニス
veil ベール
velvet ビロード、ベルベット
veneer, plywood ベニヤ
Venetian blinds ブラインド
veranda ベランダ
vest ベスト、チョッキ
veteran (expert) ベテラン
video ビデオ
video arcade ゲームセンター
video deck ビデオデッキ
Vienna ウィーン
Vietnam ベトナム
view finder ファインダー
vinyl, plastic (bag) ビニール
violin バイオリン
virus ウイルス、ビールス
visa ビザ
vitality バイタリティー
vitamin ビタミン

vocal (music) ボーカル
vodka ウォッカ
volleyball バレー、バレーボール
volt, bolt ボルト
volume (sound, amount) ボリューム
volunteer ボランティア

wafer ウエハース
Wagner ワーグナー
wagon ワゴン
Waikiki ワイキキ
waist ウエスト
waiter ウエーター
waitress ウエートレス
walking stick, cane ステッキ
Walkman ウォークマン
wall outlet, wall socket コンセント
Walter ウォルター
waltz ワルツ
Washington ワシントン
watchman, security guard ガードマン
watercress クレソン
watt ワット
wax ワックス
wedding cake ウェディングケーキ
wedding dress ウェディングドレス
western (movie, music) ウエスタン
whiskey ウイスキー
whiskey (bottle of) ボトル
whiskey (straight) ストレート
white board ホワイトボード
white clam sauce (for spaghetti) ボンゴレ
White House ホワイトハウス
white-collar worker (male) サラリーマン
windshield フロントガラス
windshield wiper ワイパー
wine ワイン
wink ウインク
wireless microphone ワイヤレスマイク
women's bust (not statue) バスト
women's lib ウーマンリブ
wonton ワンタン
wood pulp パルプ
wooden floor フローリング
wool ウール
word processor (machine) ワープロ
working experience キャリア
wrap (plastic) ラップ
wrestler レスラー

wrestling レスリング
wrestling (professional) プロレス

X-ray レントゲン

yacht, sailboat ヨット
Yamaha ヤマハ
yeast イースト
yellow pages タウンページ
yo-yo ヨーヨー
yoga ヨガ
yogurt ヨーグルト
youth hostel ユースホステル

zero ゼロ
zigzag ジグザグ
zipper ファスナー、チャック
zone ゾーン
zoom lens ズームレンズ

## JAPANESE FOR BUSY PEOPLE I & II

Association for Japanese-Language Teaching

This two-volume language-learning program makes it possible to communicate effectively in both business and social contexts.

I TEXT: ISBN 0-87011-599-5; paperback; 216 pages
  TAPES: ISBN 0-87011-637-1; four 30-minute tapes
  COMPACT DISCS: ISBN 4-7700-1607-7; two discs
  TEACHERS MANUAL: ISBN 4-7700-1608-5;
  paperback; 160 pages

II TEXT: ISBN 0-87011-919-2; paperback; 424 pages
  TAPES: ISBN 0-87011-925-7; six 60-minute tapes

## READING JAPANESE FINANCIAL NEWSPAPERS

Association for Japanese-Language Teaching

A must for business people who need direct access to the financial pages of Japanese newspapers.
ISBN 0-87011-956-7; paperback; 388 pages

## KODANSHA'S COMPACT KANJI GUIDE

A compact Japanese-English character dictionary based on the 1,945 *Jōyō* ("common use") *Kanji*. Includes 20,000 practical words.
ISBN 4-7700-1553-4; vinyl flexibinding; 928 pages

## THE COMPLETE GUIDE TO EVERYDAY KANJI

*Yaeko S. Habein and Gerald B. Mathias*

A systematic guide to remembering and understanding the 1,945 *Jōyō* ("common use") *Kanji*.
ISBN 4-7700-1509-7; paperback; 344 pages

## LET'S LEARN HIRAGANA
ISBN 0-87011-709-2; paperback; 72 pages
## LET'S LEARN KATAKANA
ISBN 0-87011-719-X; paperback; 88 pages

*Yasuko Kosaka Mitamura*

These workbooks explain in simple, clear steps how to read and write *hiragana* and *katakana*.

## JAPANESE KANA WORKBOOK

*P. G. O'Neill*

Designed to give the beginning student a systematic introduction to the *kana* and their usage.
ISBN 0-87011-039-X; paperback; 128 pages

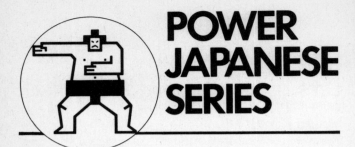

# POWER JAPANESE SERIES

---

**BEYOND POLITE JAPANESE:** A Dictionary of Japanese Slang and Colloquialisms

*Akihiko Yonekawa*

Wean yourself from the textbooks. Learn to speak more like the Japanese do.

---

**GONE FISHIN':**
New Angles on Perennial Problems

*Jay Rubin*

Clears up, with intelligence and wit, the most problematic aspects of the language.

---

**ALL ABOUT PARTICLES**

*Naoko Chino*

Discover new particles and recall the old while learning proper usage.

---

**"BODY" LANGUAGE**

*Jeffrey G. Garrison*

Have fun learning common idioms and expressions referring to the human body.

---

**INSTANT VOCABULARY THROUGH PREFIXES AND SUFFIXES**

*Timothy J. Vance*

Learn hundreds of new words by modifying your existing vocabulary.

---